P9-DCI-950

WITHDRAWN

Death Penalty

by Syd Golston

LUCENT BOOKS

A part of Gale, Cengage Learning

GALE
CENGAGE Learning·

Detroit • New York • San Francisco • New Haven, Conn • Waterville, Maine • London

© 2009 Gale, Cengage Learning

ALL RIGHTS RESERVED. No part of this work covered by the copyright herein may be reproduced, transmitted, stored, or used in any form or by any means graphic, electronic, or mechanical, including but not limited to photocopying, recording, scanning, digitizing, taping, Web distribution, information networks, or information storage and retrieval systems, except as permitted under Section 107 or 108 of the 1976 United States Copyright Act, without the prior written permission of the publisher.

Every effort has been made to trace the owners of copyrighted material.

LIBRARY OF CONGRESS CATALOGING-IN-PUBLICATION DATA

Golston, Syd.
  Death penalty / by Syd Golston.
      p. cm. -- (Hot topics)
  Includes bibliographical references and index.
  ISBN 978-1-4205-0048-6 (hardcover)
  1. Capital punishment--Juvenile literature. 2. Capital punishment--United States--Juvenile literature. I. Title.
    HV8694.G56 2009
    364.660973--dc22

                                                              2009008842

Lucent Books
27500 Drake Rd.
Farmington Hills, MI 48331

ISBN-13: 978-1-4205-0048-6
ISBN-10: 1-4205-0048-1

Printed in the United States of America
1 2 3 4 5 6 7 13 12 11 10 09

CONTENTS

FOREWORD

Young people today are bombarded with information. Aside from traditional sources such as newspapers, television, and the radio, they are inundated with a nearly continuous stream of data from electronic media. They send and receive e-mails and instant messages, read and write online "blogs," participate in chat rooms and forums, and surf the Web for hours. This trend is likely to continue. As Patricia Senn Breivik, the former dean of university libraries at Wayne State University in Detroit, has stated, "Information overload will only increase in the future. By 2020, for example, the available body of information is expected to double every 73 days! How will these students find the information they need in this coming tidal wave of information?"

Ironically, this overabundance of information can actually impede efforts to understand complex issues. Whether the topic is abortion, the death penalty, gay rights, or obesity, the deluge of fact and opinion that floods the print and electronic media is overwhelming. The news media report the results of polls and studies that contradict one another. Cable news shows, talk radio programs, and newspaper editorials promote narrow viewpoints and omit facts that challenge their own political biases. The World Wide Web is an electronic minefield where legitimate scholars compete with the postings of ordinary citizens who may or may not be well-informed or capable of reasoned argument. At times, strongly worded testimonials and opinion pieces both in print and electronic media are presented as factual accounts.

Conflicting quotes and statistics can confuse even the most diligent researchers. A good example of this is the question of whether or not the death penalty deters crime. For instance, one study found that murders decreased by nearly one-third when the death penalty was reinstated in New York in 1995. Death penalty supporters cite this finding to support their argument that the existence of the death penalty deters criminals from committing murder. However, another study found that states without the death penalty have murder rates below the national average. This study is cited by opponents of capital punishment, who reject the claim that the death penalty deters murder. Students need context and clear, informed discussion if they are to think critically and make informed decisions.

The Hot Topics series is designed to help young people wade through the glut of fact, opinion, and rhetoric so that they can think critically about controversial issues. Only by reading and thinking critically will they be able to formulate a viewpoint that is not simply the parroted views of others. Each volume of the series focuses on one of today's most pressing social issues and provides a balanced overview of the topic. Carefully crafted narrative, fully documented primary and secondary source quotes, informative sidebars, and study questions all provide excellent starting points for research and discussion. Full-color photographs and charts enhance all volumes in the series. With its many useful features, the Hot Topics series is a valuable resource for young people struggling to understand the pressing issues of the modern era.

INTRODUCTION

A FOUR-THOUSAND-YEAR-OLD DEBATE

Citizens of ancient Babylon gathered in the city's public square around the year 1750 B.C. to stare at an 8-foot-thick (2.4m) column of black stone, carved on all its sides with writing. Those who could read the words on the column pronounced for the crowd the 282 laws of the kingdom, proclaimed by Hammurabi, ruler of Babylon. Many of the laws address crimes and their consequences, which call for equal and direct revenge. Law 229 of the code reads: If a builder has built a house for a man, and has not made his work sound, and the house he built has fallen and caused the death of its owner, that builder shall be put to death.[1] Twenty-five different offenses resulted in death.

Capital punishment, the penalty of death for those judged guilty of certain extreme crimes, is as old as the earliest written history. For almost four thousand years, the death penalty has been carried out—and argued over—in societies throughout the world. Who decides which crimes are so dreadful that the guilty must be executed? Does fear of the death penalty discourage people who might commit such acts? Can the community's desire for revenge justify executions, or does that revenge make society itself more brutal? Human beings make mistakes, and what if the wrong person is put to death?

The Greeks and Romans worried less about the severity of the death penalty and more about how it would be applied among the different classes; laws were different for nobility, commoner, and slave. The Athenian lawgiver Draco believed that even lesser infractions deserved execution, and for some twenty years death was the penalty for all crimes in Athens. The Romans used methods of utmost cruelty: Depending on social status, criminals were beaten, stoned, drowned, buried alive, or crucified.

From the Middle Ages onward, England witnessed extremes of opinion toward punishment by execution. Some began to question the morality of taking a life for a life, and William the Conqueror, first king of England (A.D. 1066–1087), outlawed it altogether. The English death penalty was later restored and heavily enforced, often in the form of beheading for nobles and hanging for commoners—the word "capital" in capital punishment is derived from *capitalis*, Latin for "of the head." By the 1700s the English courts punished 222 crimes with death. These crimes included murder and kidnapping as well as such minor crimes as stealing or cutting down a neighbor's trees.

Capital punishment laws in the North American colonies reflected their British heritage. The first colonial execution was carried out at Jamestown in 1608, when George Kendall, who was accused of spying for Spain, was found guilty of treason against the settlement and hanged. All

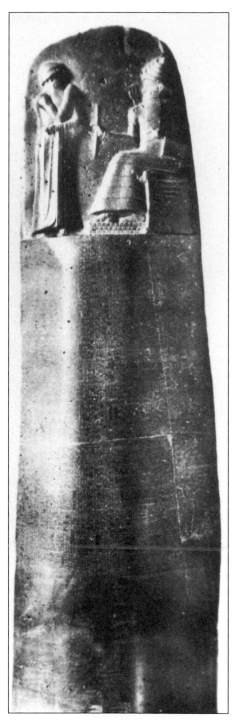

The monument of Hammurabi's Code, a stone column that contained 282 laws of the kingdom of ancient Babylon. Twenty-five of the laws resulted in the death penalty if broken.

of the colonies developed criminal codes that required capital punishment for many crimes, including murder, conspiracy, blasphemy (swearing), and witchcraft. The ill-famed Salem Witchcraft Trials of 1692 resulted in the hangings of nineteen innocent men and women.

The eighteenth-century Age of Reason in Europe produced a generation of philosophers who opposed the death penalty, and their writings affected the thinking of citizens in both the Old World and the New. One of these reflections appeared in *On Crimes and Punishment*, originally published in 1764 by Cesare Beccaria, an Italian judge who claimed that capital punishment was neither necessary nor useful. He termed it "a war of a whole nation against a citizen."[2] Beccaria thought execution was necessary only if the death of the accused could ensure the safety of the whole nation. Thomas Jefferson had read Beccaria and the other philosophers who wished to reform the criminal codes. He proposed a revision of the laws of Virginia to recommend the death penalty only for treason and murder. Jefferson's attempt was defeated in Virginia's House of Burgesses by just one vote; many legislators had shared his views.

Physician Benjamin Rush of Pennsylvania was even more opposed to capital punishment than Jefferson. He was one of the first to argue that it had a "brutalization effect" upon society, which would actually encourage more violence among citizens rather than prevent it. At the urging of Rush and Benjamin Franklin, Pennsylvania repealed the death penalty in 1794 for all offenses except murder.

Many states limited capital punishment in the nineteenth century. All the states abolished mandatory (required) death sentences for any crime. Judges and juries would have to examine each capital case individually to decide whether death would be imposed. Public hangings ceased; after the invention of electricity, some states switched to the electric chair, or later the gas chamber, which were considered more humane.

In the twentieth century, public opinion for and against the death penalty seesawed up and down depending upon current events. Eleven states abolished capital punishment between 1895 and 1917. But after the Russian Revolution in 1917 Americans feared similar revolution and socialism would spread to the United States, and the death penalty became popular once again. Most states resumed executions as a general state of suspicion spread over the country.

Fervent feelings against executions erupted again when two Italian American anarchists, Nicola Sacco and Bartolomeo Vanzetti, were executed for robbery and murder on August 23, 1927. They were later proved innocent, and 250,000 people gathered in Boston to protest their death. Criminologists wrote that capital punishment was a necessary social control during the Great Depression of the 1930s, when unemployment and desperation threatened to unravel the bonds of society.

Campaigns to end the death penalty across the United States were met with statehouse resistance. In 1972 opponents of capital punishment brought the case of *Furman v. Georgia* to the Supreme Court. In a five-to-four decision, the justices ruled that the death penalty as it was then enforced by the states violated the Eighth Amendment against cruel and unusual punishment, and all death row executions ceased. In 1976 the Court reversed itself in the case of *Gregg v. Georgia*, recognizing newer and fairer criminal codes and sentencing policies. Executions began again as some states adopted what was considered the least painful or violent method, lethal injection.

Although the number of executions in the United States has declined steadily over the past decades, supporters of the death penalty remain steadfast. Recent studies disagree over whether it deters criminals, but some evidence supports its value in preventing crime. Many Americans still believe in the principles of Hammurabi's Code and of the Bible: "an eye for an eye, a tooth for a tooth." Support continues for revenge against the most horrible of crimes.

Other Americans oppose capital punishment on many grounds. They cite the old Enlightenment philosophies about unfairness, failure to prevent crime, and the evils of executing the wrong defendant. They note that 129 nations have abolished capital punishment, including most of the advanced industrial countries, and only 68 continue to enforce it.

Recent protest has centered on the methods of execution. The Supreme Court heard oral arguments for and against the use of

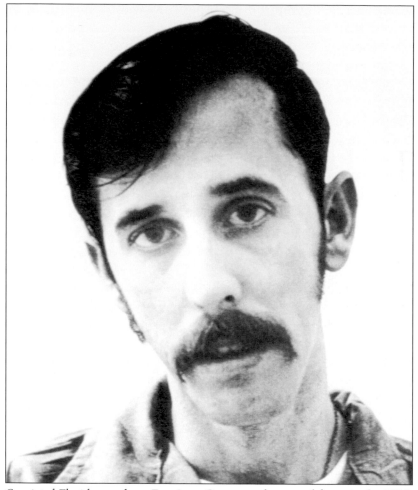

Convicted Florida murderer Troy Leon Gregg was the central figure in the 1976 U.S. Supreme Court case Gregg v. Georgia.

lethal injection on January 7, 2008, in the Kentucky case of *Baze v. Rees*, and the justices' decision denied that the practice of lethal injection comprised cruel and unusual punishment, permitting the continuation of executions in the states.

Internationally, nations such as China, Iran, Saudi Arabia, and Pakistan join the United States in filling the world's death rows. At the same time, organizations like the United Nations and Amnesty International work against it.

An agonizing four-thousand-year-old debate continues.

THE HISTORY OF THE DEATH PENALTY

The use of capital punishment can be traced to the beginnings of recorded history. Over time, the practice of putting to death those who most seriously offend society has been refined and limited—but it persists today, even though most of the world's nations have abolished it.

The Earliest Civilizations

"An eye for an eye, and a tooth for a tooth." Four books of the Hebrew Bible include this citation. The Book of Leviticus contains the most direct reference to a civil death penalty, in this divine proclamation to Moses: "If a man takes the life of any human being, he shall surely be put to death. . . . If a man injures his neighbor, just as he has done, so it shall be done to him. Fracture for fracture, eye for eye, tooth for tooth; just as he has injured a man, so it shall be inflicted on him."[3] In western cultures, that concept of equal retribution for taking a life became the basis for thousands of years of public policy on capital punishment.

The Old Testament prescribes the penalty of death for dozens of misdeeds other than murder. Many of these seem like minor offenses for such an extreme punishment: trying to convert an Israelite to another religion, attempting to communicate with the dead, adultery, sexual activity before marriage, and even cursing one's parents. A common execution method described in the Bible is stoning to death. In reality, few were executed because the standards of proof were so high. Even a murder verdict required not one but two eyewitnesses.

Biblical scholars are careful to point out that this advice was given to the Israelites as a society, not to individuals who would

Stoning to death was a common execution method in biblical times, as shown in this illustration of St. Stephen's stoning.

create mayhem by carrying out their personal revenge. It was perhaps the first societal policy we can trace in the ancient world, although some evidence suggests that the Chinese had law codes that included capital punishment before 2200 B.C.

The Babylonian Code of Hammurabi from 1750 B.C. is the first dated evidence of a state's statutory use of the death penalty. Along with causing another's death, many kinds of illicit sexual acts were capital crimes in Babylon. So were thefts from the royal treasury, selling stolen goods, kidnapping, hiding a fugitive slave, and disorderly conduct in a tavern. In all, there were twenty-five laws in the code that called for the death penalty. Certain offenses called for specific methods of execution; sexual offenders were drowned, and burglars were hanged from a "gibbet," a pole with a noose set up at the scene of the crime.

Capital punishment also existed in ancient China, according to the writings of Confucius (551–479 B.C.) and his followers. Confucians believed more in the power of the virtuous example to deter criminal behavior than in the sanction of punishment, but they also recognized the occasional justification for the death penalty. They opposed the more barbaric death penalties of the time, sawing in half and boiling to death among them.

The Greeks in Homer's time, around 800 B.C., acted upon the urge for retaliation for a homicide. The victim's family caught and killed the murderer, or accepted a "blood price"—a payment for the death that would restore peace and satisfy the aggrieved family.

Draco's Code in ancient Athens, recorded in 621 B.C., punished even trivial crimes with death and is the source of the term "draconian," which means "overly severe." It was said that Draco's laws were written in blood. The civil laws were also intolerably strict, such as the punishment of enslavement for nonpayment of debts.

The Athenian leader Solon replaced Draco's Code twenty-five years later with a much more lenient system that prescribed the death penalty only for crimes that endangered the entire community, and offered banishment from Athens forever to defendants who admitted their guilt. These Athenian statutes remained in place with few changes for more than two hundred years. They were carried out in a hierarchy of justice courts, set up to try different degrees of crimes, including a separate court for repeat killers. Aristotle wrote that those repeat offenders had to defend themselves from a boat so they would not contaminate the members of the court, who were seated at the water's edge. The most famous of all Athenian trials resulted in the execution of the philosopher Socrates in 399 B.C.

The Romans' Laws of the Twelve Tables (circa 450 B.C.) named capital punishment for several crimes, most of them forms of murder, including poisoning and assassination. Murder within the family was punished most cruelly. The later *lex Cornelia* (Cornelian Law) said that "he who killed a father or mother, grandfather or grandmother, was punished by being whipped till he bled, sewn up in a sack with a dog, cock, viper, and ape, and thrown into the sea."[4]

Slaves and foreigners under the Romans suffered at the hands of the law more severely than Roman citizens. A slave could be tortured, for instance. Execution by crucifixion was reserved for noncitizens who had committed the worst crimes; the suffering of Christ was standard procedure, including whipping and carrying the cross to the site of execution. Victims who were nailed to the cross actually died of asphyxiation, while those who were bound to it died of starvation, some surviving as long as nine days.

The Islamic laws of the Koran were recorded in the seventh century A.D. and included capital punishment for many crimes, including robbery, adultery, and religious crimes. Oddly, murder was not mentioned among them; murder was to be treated as a civil crime between families and decided by the relatives of the victim, who could choose death or retribution payment.

The Middle Ages

Roman Catholic Christianity became the most important institution in Europe in the Middle Ages, from around the fifth to the fifteenth centuries. In medieval European societies the death penalty was often inflicted for violations of faith, and church officials decided what qualified as a violation of faith. The laws of this era provided for the execution of witches, sorcerers, nonbelievers, and heretics (those who did not conform with the official

Socrates of Ancient Athens

The Athenian philosopher Socrates (470–399 B.C.) was known as "the gadfly of Athens" because of his unrelenting style of intellectual investigation. He questioned the ancestral gods and the process of democracy itself, claiming that in no other craft would the craftsmen be chosen by popular vote. His ideas about virtue challenged the concept of the will of the gods.

Socrates' disciples included Alcibiades and Critias, both of whom betrayed Athenian democracy in favor of its enemy Sparta, and this association led many to think that the philosopher's influence on young leaders threatened the state.

Socrates was accused of corrupting the youth of Athens and disbelieving in the gods. A jury of some five hundred freeborn male citizen volunteers, selected by lottery, was called to decide the case; a guilty verdict required only a majority of the jurors. Socrates was condemned by just over half the jury.

After their first verdict, a second was called to decide Socrates' penalty. The prosecutor asked for death, and the jury agreed. In accordance with his long-held ideas of obeying the law, the philosopher carried out his execution by his own hand, drinking a bowl of hemlock which would kill him.

Greek philosopher Socrates prepares to carry out his own death sentence by drinking poisonous hemlock.

teachings of the church). The Cathars in France and the Hussites in the Czech region were burned at the stake for their contrary religious beliefs.

The most famous heretic to suffer this fate was Joan of Arc, a teenage peasant girl who claimed that visions of the saints called her to lead the French army and drive the English from France during the Hundred Years' War. Dressed in men's armor, Joan led the French triumphantly at Orléans in 1429. The English captured her just a year later and tried her as a heretic.

EYE FOR EYE, TOOTH FOR TOOTH

"If a man takes the life of any human being, he shall surely be put to death. . . . If a man injures his neighbor, just as he has done, so it shall be done to him." —Leviticus 24:17–20.

Clergy who supported the English found Joan guilty of claiming false divine revelations, of immodesty in wearing male clothes, and even of making incorrect claims that the saints spoke French rather than English. On May 30, 1431, Joan was tied to a pillar in the marketplace of Rouen. Holding a small wooden cross, she called the names of her saints as the flames grew higher. According to the legend of Joan of Arc, her beating heart was found in the ashes, which were then burned again.

In the later Middle Ages, the Catholic Church set up Inquisition bodies in several states, intended to root out heresy and execute people who refused to repent; the most violent of these was the Spanish Inquisition. Tomás de Torquemada, the Spanish grand inquisitor, was infamous for the use of torture to convert heretics, but historians estimate that more than five thousand prisoners resisted such tactics and were burned at the stake.

Protestants were just as likely to put their religious enemies to death. In Henry VIII's England (1509–1547), some seventy-two thousand people were executed. When Henry broke with Rome, he founded his own Anglican church and seized monasteries all over England. Catholics in the north protested the

Joan of Arc is burned at the stake on May 30, 1431, after clergy found her guilty of several charges, most prominently claiming false divine revelations.

seizures in what was known as the Pilgrimage of Grace. Henry received the protesters, heard their petitions, and sent them home—where they were arrested, tried for treason, and hanged. Reginald Pole, the last Catholic archbishop of Canterbury, wrote to Henry, "Thy butcheries and horrible executions have made England the slaughterhouse of innocence."[5]

The Modern Era

Executions for common crimes in Europe were profuse in the seventeenth and eighteenth centuries. By the 1700s, 222 crimes were punishable by death, including stealing a sheep, cutting

The Guillotine and the Reign of Terror

The most infamous executions in history took place in Paris during ten months of the French Revolution that are called the "Reign of Terror." Some say as many as eighteen thousand people were executed, mostly in ghastly and crowded public spectacles.

The French Revolution began in 1789 as a movement to wrest power from the court of King Louis XVI and place it in the hands of an elected national assembly. Immediate violence erupted; in Paris ordinary citizens attacked the Bastille fortress to get their hands on firearms, and in the countryside peasants revolted and stormed the manors of their landlords.

Louis XVI was tried for crimes against the people of France and be-headed by the guillotine in January 1793. Members of the radical Jacobin political party, under their extremist leader Maximilien Robespierre, formed a committee of public safety and began to eliminate their enemies.

Queen Marie Antoinette was found guilty of treason and paraded in an open cart through the streets of Paris to her beheading. Thousands shared her fate during the Terror, with arrests, trials, and executions orchestrated by Robespierre. Anybody suspected of opposing the revolution was swiftly tried and sent to the guillotine. In a final reaction to the horrific violence, legislators turned on Robespierre himself. On July 27, 1794, Robespierre and twenty-one of his followers were guillotined.

down a tree, and robbing a rabbit warren. Eventually, many judges considered death penalties for such crimes excessive, and other penalties came into use. The justices commuted sentences to imprisonment and deportation, often to English penal colonies in Australia and the American colony of Georgia.

For centuries, a prisoner could escape the gallows through "benefit of clergy." If he could prove that he was a member of the church, a priest, a monk, or even a nonordained cleric, he could be set free. The only way to know for certain that the defendant was indeed such a member of a religious order was to ask him to read out loud, as churchmen were the only literate members of society. If the defendant read from the Bible successfully, he was spared.

The eighteenth-century philosophical movement called the Enlightenment brought about a questioning of superstition and the traditional values of the Middle Ages, replacing tradition with human reason as the arbiter of right and wrong in society. Optimism and reform replaced fear and punishment in western Europe and in the English colonies as well. Thinkers like Jean-Jacques Rousseau, Voltaire, and Denis Diderot in France; John Locke, Jeremy Bentham, and David Hume in England; and Thomas Jefferson, Thomas Paine, and Benjamin Franklin in the colonies began to challenge the value and even the morality of capital punishment.

Cesare Beccaria, born into a noble family in Milan in 1738, wrote his treatise called *On Crimes and Punishments* in 1764. Beccaria rejected the death penalty's ability to deter criminals, believing that life imprisonment was more dreaded by the populace. He wrote that society brutalized itself by inflicting capital punishment: "The punishment of death is pernicious to society, from the example of barbarity it affords. . . . Is it not absurd, that the laws, which detest and punish homicide, should, in order to prevent murder, publicly commit murder themselves?"[6] Beccaria recognized only one situation in which capital punishment was appropriate: when the criminal, although deprived of his liberty and imprisoned, still has the power and connections to upset a nation's security and foment a revolution.

Enlightenment Influences Early United States

The American colonies had followed their English motherland on matters of capital punishment, but leaders in the new nation were profoundly affected by Enlightenment philosophy and brought about new ideas. Beccaria's work was admired by Benjamin Franklin, Thomas Jefferson, and Benjamin Rush (a fellow signer of the Declaration of Independence).

Jefferson's bill to repeal the death penalty in Virginia for all crimes except murder and treason was defeated by just one vote.

In 1794 Pennsylvania became the first state in the new union to abolish the death penalty for all crimes except first-degree murder. Pennsylvania had already passed laws establishing degrees of guilt for taking another's life. The Quaker population in Pennsylvania was a guiding influence in reforming capital punishment. Quaker teachings forbid taking another's life.

During the French Revolution of 1789–1794, tens of thousands of executions took place. One of the more famous ones was that of King Louis XVI, who was beheaded by guillotine after being found guilty of "charges against the people of France."

While the new United States took steps to limit capital punishment at the end of the eighteenth century, France experienced a frenzy of capital punishment. The French Revolution in 1789 brought about a bloodbath of executions in the jaws of the guillotine. Some say as many as eighteen thousand people were executed during a ten-month period called the Reign of Terror.

Most European nations and the United States built better prisons in the early nineteenth century and reduced the number of capital crimes and the number of actual executions. England's 222 capital crimes were cut by nearly half. Public executions, formerly thought to serve as a deterrent to future criminals, were attacked as grisly spectacles and occasions of drunkenness, fighting, and obscenity. They were replaced by executions in prisons.

Michigan was the first state to end the death penalty for all crimes except treason, followed by Rhode Island and Wisconsin. When states that kept capital punishment got rid of mandatory sentences, people considered it a great reform step forward: Judges would decide, based on specific circumstances of a crime, whether it warranted the extreme punishment.

However, most states kept the death penalty and used it. Southern states increased the number of capital crimes, especially those committed by slaves. Slave uprisings in the 1820s and 1830s resulted in wholesale executions.

Death penalty reformers were often abolitionists, and until the end of the Civil War and the Reconstruction, reform energy was spent on getting rid of slavery and not on capital punishment issues. By the turn of the twentieth century, prison and sentencing reform were back on the agenda; Maine, Iowa, and Kansas eliminated capital punishment. Following the harnessing of electricity, electrocution replaced hanging and firing squads as the method of execution in many states. The first criminal to die in the electric chair was William Kemmler, executed in 1890 in New York state.

Support for Execution Fluctuates in America

The reformers' efforts returned with the Progressive Era, from the 1890s until World War I (1914–1918). Capital punishment reform

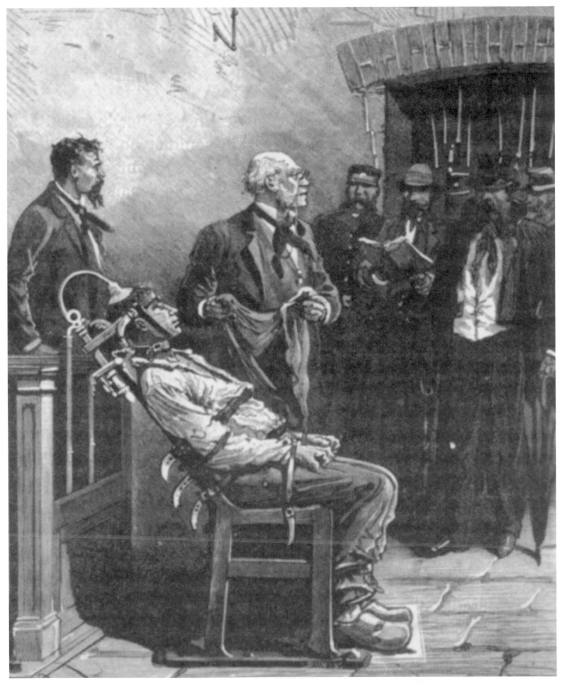

In the late 1800s, the electric chair became the preferred method of capital punishment in the United States.

joined a long list of movements aiming to improve American society, including labor unions, women's suffrage, slum clearance, prohibition of alcohol, and cleaning up political corruption. At the outbreak of World War I and the Russian Revolution of 1914, fear of class conflict and radical immigrants changed attitudes toward capital punishment, which returned in most of the states that had abolished it during the Progressive period.

More executions occurred during the Great Depression of the 1930s than at any other time in American history, an average of 167 per year. Many feared that the American capitalist system itself might be overthrown unless the poor and unemployed, and their radical champions, the left-wing Socialists and Communists, were controlled and punished by ever-vigilant authorities.

EXECUTION DOES NOT SERVE THE GREATER GOOD

"[Punishment of death is] a war of a whole nation against a citizen whose destruction they consider as necessary, or useful to the general good. But if I can . . . demonstrate that it is neither necessary nor useful, I shall have gained the cause of humanity." —Cesare Beccaria, Italian judge.

Cesare Beccaria, "Of the Punishment of Death," chap. 28, in *On Crimes and Punishments* (originally published in Italian, 1764). Philadelphia: R. Bell, 1778. www.constitution.org/cb/crim_pun.htm.

The Soviet Union was an ally of the United States during World War II (1939–1945), but following the war, a second "Red Scare" led by Senator Joseph McCarthy whipped up paranoid fears of Soviet spies in every corner of the U.S. government. In an atmosphere of hysterical anticommunism, Governor Allan Shivers of Texas actually suggested that death be the penalty for mere membership in the Communist Party.[7]

During the Cold War, a period of ongoing political tension between the United States and the Soviets that lasted from 1945 to 1991, a handful of spies were prosecuted and executed for passing secrets to the Soviets.

The Case of Sacco and Vanzetti

On April 15, 1920, two paymasters from a factory in South Braintree, Massachusetts, were gunned down and over $15,000 in cash boxes was grabbed. Both gunmen jumped into a waiting car, and the bandit gang sped away from their pursuers.

Three weeks later, two Italian immigrants were arrested for the crime. Nicola Sacco and Bartolomeo Vanzetti were not originally suspects, but at the time of their arrest they were both carrying guns, they were active members of a radical anarchist group, and both of them lied during questioning to protect their political comrades.

Anarchists believed in overthrow of all central government, by violence if necessary. Their history as political agitators in strikes and demonstrations severely damaged Sacco and Vanzetti's chances for a fair trial. They were found guilty of murder in the Boston courtroom of Judge Webster Thayer in 1921.

Six years of hearings and appeals followed. A bank robber named Madeiros confessed to the Braintree payroll murders; there was also evidence from many quarters that the notorious local Morelli Gang had organized the crime.

The Sacco and Vanzetti case became a rallying cry for those opposed to the death penalty, including future Supreme Court justice Felix Frankfurter, then a Harvard law professor. Millions saw it as a miscarriage of social justice. The governor of Massachusetts appointed a review committee, called the Lowell Committee because it included Harvard's president Abbott Lowell, but the committee supported the original verdict.

Protesters around the world held vigils for them, but Sacco and Vanzetti were executed in the electric chair on August 27, 1927.

Many people felt the Sacco and Vanzetti case was a miscarriage of justice.

Although the majority of U.S. citizens support the death penalty, the number of citizens who oppose it continues to grow.

Support for the death penalty in the United States and in countries around the world waned throughout the late twentieth century. Eighty-six nations no longer use capital punishment; most of them outlawed it in the final decades of the twentieth century. Few countries now have public executions; more humane methods are used in most executions, with notable exceptions in Saudi Arabia, which still beheads some offenders, and in Iran, where three people have been stoned to death between 2007 and 2009. The Amnesty International organization has called these executions "grotesque and horrific,"[8] and called on the Iranian government to stop the practice.

The movement to abolish executions has been aided by Hollywood movies such as *Cell 2455 Death Row* (1955), *In Cold Blood* (1967), *Kill Me If You Can: The Caryl Chessman Story* (1977), *Dead Man Walking* (1995), and *Monster* (2003). Organizations and attorneys also mounted a series of legal challenges in the courts. Since 1973, 127 prisoners on death row have been exonerated, including 16 whose cases were cleared based on DNA evidence.

In the United States a majority of citizens continue to support capital punishment, even as opposition to it builds strength. An ABC News–sponsored poll in 2007 showed that just over 60 percent of Americans favor the death penalty, down from 77 percent just a decade ago; and "support for the death penalty slips further, to just under half of the public, when life in prison without parole is offered as an alternative."[9]

Since 1976, 1,099 convicted murderers have been executed, 85 percent of them by lethal injection. The 2008 Supreme Court case *Baze vs. Rees* called into question the legality of lethal injection as a "cruel and unusual punishment" in violation of the Eighth Amendment to the Constitution. Some believed that the Court's decision would reshape the states' use of capital punishment, but the Court ruled to permit lethal injection executions.

ARGUMENTS FOR THE DEATH PENALTY

Death penalty proponents have cited reasons like retribution and deterrence for centuries. However, when the Information Age enabled the systematic gathering of large amounts of data, differing statistical interpretations emerged: For instance, one set of data indicates that capital punishment deters violent crime, while another set can be used to show that it does not.

Retribution

This justification for capital punishment is one of principle and dates back to the earliest philosophies of justice: Certain horrible crimes should be punished with equal violence in order to uphold the values of society. This reasoning suggests the death penalty is a moral necessity. The concept of retribution extends beyond the need for revenge by victims' families; in fact, it channels what might be destructive acts of personal revenge into a controlled way to deal with anger and loss.

The counterargument to retribution as a moral imperative that enforces respect for the sanctity of life is the claim that capital punishment brutalizes society—that committing murder to avenge murder leads to less respect for life, not more. This side of the debate says that if the government represents all the members of society, then every member of society is individually responsible and accountable when someone is executed. This is an argument that dates back to Beccaria's eighteenth-century writings in *On Crimes and Punishments*.

Public Support

A significant majority of Americans support capital punishment.[10] Thirty-seven elected state legislatures have passed capital punishment

Adolf Eichmann: Society Seeks Retribution

Karl Adolf Eichmann served with Hitler's SS forces at the Dachau Concentration Camp and then rose quickly in the ranks to become the director of the Gestapo's Department for Jewish Affairs, directly responsible for the deportation of over 3 million Jews to death camps. After the defeat of the Nazi regime, he escaped from an American prison camp and hid in Argentina for ten years until Israeli agents captured him and brought him to trial in Jerusalem. Eichmann's trial re-aired the horrors of the Holocaust and society's responsibility to punish the evil among us. He was executed on May 31, 1962.

Moshe Landau, the presiding judge who sentenced Eichmann, said, "After considering the appropriate sentence for the Accused with a deep feeling of the burden of responsibility borne by us, we reached the conclusion that in order to punish the Accused and deter others, the maximum penalty laid down in the law must be imposed on him. In the Judgment we described the crimes in which the Accused took part. They are of unparalleled horror in their nature and their scope."

Quoted in Nizkor Project, "Trial of Adolf Eichmann, Record of the Proceedings in the District Court of Jerusalem," State of Israel Ministry of Justice. www .nizkor.org/hweb/people/e/eichmann-adolf/transcripts/.

Nazi war criminal Adolf Eichmann appears at his trial in 1961. He was convicted of crimes relating to the Holocaust and was executed on May 31, 1962.

laws. Death penalty advocates say these laws should not be nullified by a Supreme Court decision. In a democracy, the will of the people must count.

Opponents answer this argument by citing eras in American history like the Red Scare and the Cold War when fear instead of thoughtful analysis shaped public policy. Majorities in American history have made choices that, in hindsight, seem wrong.

Deterrence

The most common argument in favor of capital punishment is that it stops possible criminals because they fear their own death if they are caught. Studies of murder rates from states which have the death penalty and use it, those who have it on the books but do not execute killers, and states which have abolished capital punishment have led to confusing conclusions.

MURDERERS DESERVE DEATH

"The punishment of murderers has been earned by the pain and suffering they have imposed on their victims." —Dudley Sharp, vice president of Justice for All.

Dudley Sharp, "Do We Need the Death Penalty? It Is Just and Right." *The World and I*, September 2002.

Some recent studies show that fear of the death penalty deters criminals. One study in 2006 by economists Hashem Dezhbakhsh and Joanna M. Shepherd examined each of the fifty states individually from 1960 to 2000; they reported that having the death penalty on the books deters capital crimes and that actually holding executions increases that effect.[11] The state of Illinois suspended executions from 2000–2003, and just before he left office in 2003, the governor commuted all the death row inmates' sentences to life imprisonment. Economics researcher Dale O. Cloninger and professor of finance Roberto Marchesini examined the four years in Illinois without capital punishment and found an increase of 150 homicides during that period.[12]

Some researchers question the methods and samplings used in studies that support deterrence. These researchers point to other reports that show murder rates are unconnected to whether a state has or uses the death penalty. The Death Penalty Information Center reports that "Consistent with previous years, the 2006 FBI Uniform Crime Report showed that the South had the highest murder rate. The South accounts for over 80% of executions. The Northeast, which has less than 1% of all executions, again had the lowest murder rate."[13]

Critics also claim that murder is committed by human beings who are mentally disturbed and cannot weigh consequences in a sane and serious way, so the possibility of their own executions would not change their actions. However, capital crimes such as treason and assassination are planned by those who do calculate the consequences, and who might be deterred by the death penalty. That possibility was a factor in the sentencing of Julius and Ethel Rosenberg, nuclear weapons spies from the 1950s.

The Rosenbergs: Death Penalty for Traitors

The Cold War between the Soviet Union and the United States followed World War II. When the Soviets developed their own nuclear weapons in just four years after the United States used atomic bombs at Hiroshima and Nagasaki, the belief was widespread that traitor scientists in the United States must have leaked secrets to the Russians.

Julius Rosenberg was indeed such an informant. Rosenberg passed hundreds of technical reports to Soviet agents, and some evidence indicated that he recruited other spies who were sympathetic to the Communist cause. Ethel Rosenberg helped her husband to compile the notes containing atomic secrets that Julius gave to his Soviet contacts.

The Rosenbergs' trial began on March 6, 1951, and they were soon convicted under the Espionage Act. Both of the Rosenbergs were sent to the electric chair at Sing Sing Prison in New York on June 19, 1953. They were the only two American civilians ever to be executed for espionage during the Cold War. Especially in Ethel Rosenberg's case, it was clear that in the fearful and accusatory atmosphere of the Cold War, a prime motive for their

Ethel Rosenberg and her husband, Julius Rosenberg, were accused of passing atomic secrets to Soviet agents following World War II. The two were convicted of treason and executed in the electric chair on June 19, 1953.

sentences was deterrence. Authors Ronald Radosh and Joyce Milton state, "There was the very real desire to frighten other individuals who might potentially lend themselves to such activities in the future."[14]

Research on deterrence is still inconclusive. Many who favor the death penalty recognize that conclusions differ. They feel that until better and more definitive evidence is found, it is better to continue executing criminals. As John McAdams, political scientist at Marquette University, explains, "If we execute murderers and there is in fact no deterrent effect, we have killed a bunch of murderers. If we fail to execute murderers, and doing so would in fact have deterred other murders, we have allowed the killing of a bunch of innocent victims. I would much rather risk the former. This, to me, is not a tough call."[15]

Opponents collect studies that show no deterrence value to capital punishment. Canada, for instance, has not executed anyone since 1962 but has not experienced any increase in capital crime rates.

According to the American Civil Liberties Union, "The vast preponderance of the evidence shows that the death penalty is no more effective than imprisonment in deterring murder and that it may even be an incitement to criminal violence. Death-penalty states as a group do not have lower rates of criminal homicide than non-death-penalty states."[16]

Protection of Society from Repeat Killers

Some criminals will never be rehabilitated. If they are imprisoned for life, they may become eligible for parole and commit additional murders. Some prisoners serving time for murder were previously convicted of another murder; if those prisoners had been executed the first time, lives would have been saved. Some people argue that protection of these new victims should be more important than the rights of convicted killers.

Another argument is that imprisoning murderers puts other prison inmates and guards at risk. Death penalty advocates believe that some killers must be executed to save others in their presence. Even lifetime imprisonment might not be a safe choice for some convicts, such as Jack Henry Abbott.

Famous Reprieves

John Smith, English burglar, 1705: John Smith was hanged at Tyburn gallows on December 12, 1705. He had been hanging for fifteen minutes when a runner arrived, and as the crowd shouted "Reprieve!" he was cut down and revived. Even though the reprieve turned out to be an elaborately staged hoax, he was legitimately pardoned and became a celebrity speaker. The story of "Half-Hanged Smith" comes from the *Newgate Calendar*, a sensationalist publication describing the crimes, trials, and executions of common criminals from Newgate Prison in London, intended as a moral lesson to the population.

Fyodor Dostoyevsky, Russian novelist, 1849: Dostoyevsky and his friends were sentenced to death by firing squad for subversive political activities. On the morning of December 22, 1849, as their hands were being bound for execution, a reprieve arrived from Czar Nicholas I. Instead of being shot, the men were to be deported to Siberia, where they would serve four years in a labor camp. Dostoyevsky went on to write some of the greatest novels in all literature.

Russian prisoner, 1880s: Czar Alexander III wrote the death sentence of a prisoner in his own handwriting: "Pardon impossible, to be sent to Siberia." His Danish wife the Czarina Dagmar believed the prisoner was innocent. She saved his life by transposing the comma in the message so that it read, "Pardon, impossible to be sent to Siberia."

Jack Henry Abbott: Repeat Murderer

Jack Henry Abbott's early life was a common criminal story: He was an abused child who grew up in foster care, juvenile detention homes, and reform school. At age twenty-one he was serving a sentence for forgery in a Utah prison when he stabbed another inmate to death. He was given an additional three to twenty-three years for the killing and then escaped to Colorado, where he was apprehended in a bank robbery.

Abbott read about *The Executioner's Song*, Norman Mailer's book about death row murderer Gary Gilmore, and began a long correspondence with Mailer. His brilliantly written letters about prison life were published by Mailer as *In the Belly of the Beast*, and several celebrities supported Abbott's parole in 1981. However, prison officials at the parole hearing testified to their fear that the

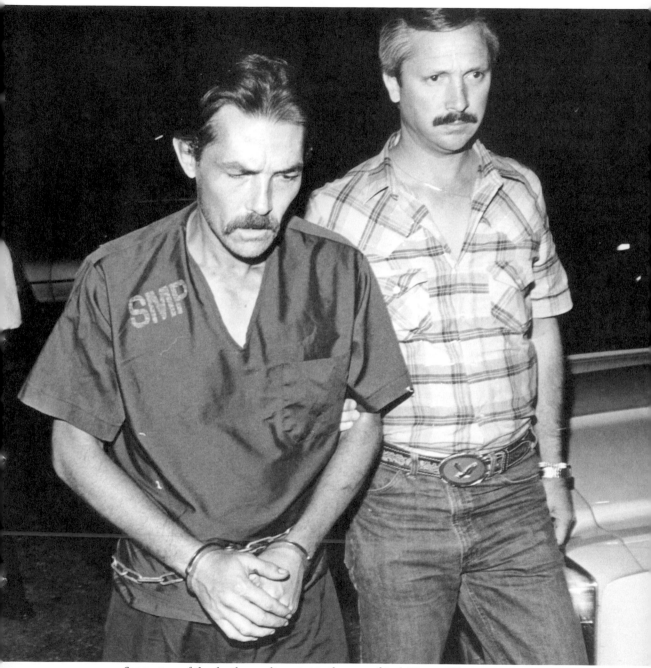

Supporters of the death penalty point to the case of Jack Henry Abbott, an inmate convicted of murder but who was eventually released on parole. Abbott committed murder again, only six weeks after being released from prison.

killer was still a dangerous psychotic. Nonetheless, Abbott was released.

Just six weeks after he was released from prison, Abbott got into a trivial argument in a Manhattan restaurant and stabbed a man to death once again. He escaped but was apprehended several months later. In 2002 he hanged himself in his cell, but he never repented for the murders he committed.

Reduction of Violence During Other Felonies

Many death row criminals have committed "felony murders," that is, killings that occurred during the commission of another crime, such as rape or burglary. If a victim dies in the course of a felony, whether or not the killer intended that death to occur, the defendant is guilty of first-degree murder and may be sentenced to death. For instance, if an arsonist burns down a building and someone sleeping inside the building dies, the arsonist can be convicted of first-degree murder and executed.

The argument is made that felons would kill even more victims as they committed crimes if there were no felony murder executions. With capital punishment hanging over their heads, criminals will not risk an escalation into violence; especially, they will not shoot the police who arrest them. The opposition viewpoint to this claim is that few criminals really contemplate the consequences of getting caught.

Costs of Life Imprisonment vs. Execution

The expense of keeping a prisoner alive for the rest of his life is often considered a powerful argument for execution over imprisonment without parole. It seems to be a waste of taxpayers' money to feed, clothe, and supervise

Many studies show that life imprisonment is actually less expensive than execution.

society's worst citizens; this is money that could be better spent on preventing crime through police work or education.

However, dozens of state reports show that it actually costs more to execute a prisoner than it does to keep him alive for forty, fifty, or more years. A Duke University study found that "the death penalty costs North Carolina $2.16 million per execution over the costs of a non–death penalty murder case with a sentence of imprisonment for life."[17]

EXECUTION IS JUST FOR THOSE WHO STEAL LIVES

"If a man steals your bicycle and society allows him to keep and ride around on the bicycle, most of us would find that profoundly unjust. Why, then, is it just to allow everyone who steals a life to keep his own? The answer is that it is not just." —Dennis Prager, columnist and radio talk show host.

Dennis Prager, *Milwaukee Journal Sentinel: JS Online*, June 9, 2001. www.jsonline.com.

Capital punishment is so expensive because death row facilities, with their increased security and requirements for isolation from other prisoners, cost more than other prisons. However, the courtroom legal costs for repeated appeals of the sentence account for the majority of the expense. Advocates of the death penalty find the cost arguments in favor of life imprisonment unacceptable. They point out that if the abolitionists did not file so many appeals, the cost of execution would go down. Advocates also argue that the cost is less important than the state's ability to provide justice.

Protection of Defendants' Rights

In the United States very few convicted murderers are sentenced to die—approximately one in every fifty. Even in states where an elected judge does the sentencing and would be more likely to impose capital punishment to be "tough on crime," only two in fifty convicted killers receive the death penalty. Murderers on death row who are actually executed represent a much lower proportion, 0.2 percent, or about one in five hundred.

Death penalty advocates point to the many processes in place that protect the rights of the defendant in capital cases and work to reduce or reverse death sentences. If any procedural errors from the original trial can be substantiated on appeal, the accused receives a new trial.

Summary of Proponents' Arguments

The death penalty is warranted, according to its supporters, for the following reasons:

1. *Retribution.* To take a moral stance against evil acts, society must punish its worst offenders with death.

2. *Public support.* In polls, the majority of Americans favor use of the death penalty.

3. *Deterrence.* Although studies seem contradictory, some research shows that use of capital punishment deters criminals from committing murders.

4. *Protection of society from repeat killers.* If they had been executed the first time, the other victims of repeat murderers would never have died.

5. *Reduction of violence during other felonies.* Fear of the death penalty stops felons from murdering victims and police officers.

6. *Cost.* The money used to jail murderers for life is better spent on protection and education.

7. *Defendants' rights and rarity of executions.* Safeguards of killers' rights and elaborate appeal procedures lead to the execution of only a tiny fraction of murderers.

8. *Reprieves.* Even when all other procedures have not stopped an execution, clemency by the governor, the president, or the Supreme Court is possible.

Harris County, Texas, home to the city of Houston, invokes the death penalty more frequently than any other county in the United States. Harris County offers the following safeguards to the accused: A grand jury must indict the accused on murder charges; a panel of judges must determine that the death penalty is possible in the case; attorneys must be assigned to the defendant whether or not he or she can afford them; money is awarded for the costs of investigating the case; the burden of proof beyond a reasonable doubt is on the prosecution; and all twelve jurors must unanimously find the defendant guilty.

A separate sentencing phase begins once a guilty verdict is chosen. Mitigating circumstances are presented at that time; these are conditions of the case and the defendant, such as poverty, child abuse, emotional or mental problems, or lack of a prior record, that can lessen the punishment. Whatever the sentence, the accused receives an automatic first appeal.

These procedures are standard around the United States. Opponents of capital punishment respond by citing inmates on death row whose innocence has been established by new DNA or other evidence, but who were convicted despite these safeguards.

Reprieves

At the final hour, governors may grant a reprieve for a convict about to be executed. Proponents of the death penalty cite the commuted sentences of death row inmates as a final protection against unwarranted executions. In many states review boards examine each case and recommend to the governor which prisoners should be offered clemency (reprieve).

Texas prisoner Kenneth Foster was just seven hours away from a lethal injection when Governor Rick Perry took the recommendation of the Texas Board of Pardons and Paroles, which had voted six to one to commute Foster's sentence to life imprisonment. Foster was the getaway driver in a 1996 robbery. His partner shot the victim as Foster sat ninety feet away. Texas has a "Law of Parties" that considers those who had a major role in a capital crime as guilty as the actual killer. Newspapers around the state ran editorials calling for Foster's reprieve, citing too many Texas executions: twenty-one in the first half of 2007, and four hundred in the state since the reinstatement of the death penalty in 1982.

In Connecticut, Georgia, and Idaho, a review board by itself may grant a reprieve, and in Nebraska, Nevada, and Utah, the governor sits on the board that decides upon clemency. The Supreme Court and the president of the United States can also grant reprieves. In the 1974 case of *Schick v. Reed*, the Supreme Court upheld the right of the president to grant not only a reprieve but the conditions that would accompany it (in the *Schick* case, life imprisonment without parole).

OBJECTIONS TO THE DEATH PENALTY

Most arguments against the death penalty are more recent than those that support it. The study of society, called sociology, which is only about two hundred years old, has produced many of those arguments. Criminology, a branch of sociology, focuses often on the effects of capital punishment. As with claims supporting the death penalty, each argument attacking it also elicits opposing responses.

Brutalization Effect

Some opponents go so far as to call the effect of executions "barbarous." Public violence, they say, encourages the disturbed citizens of society to commit more violence. For example, in the aftermath of the assassination of President John F. Kennedy, homicide rates rose. Terrorists and mass killers like Timothy McVeigh may actually be encouraged by the prospect of public execution; they desire the additional publicity for their causes that comes when they are executed. They may also seek self-importance as martyrs to those causes.

Beccaria wrote in 1764 that the death penalty reduces the sensitivity of all of us to human suffering. Opponents believe that even if deaths were physically painless (and many examples of gruesome electrocutions and hangings gone awry can be found), institutionalized murder causes psychological trauma to everyone in society.

According to the ACLU:

A society that respects life does not deliberately kill human beings. An execution is a violent public spectacle of official homicide, and one that endorses killing to solve social problems—the worst possible example to set for the citizenry. Governments worldwide have often attempted to justify their lethal fury by extolling the purported benefits that such killing would bring to the rest of society. The benefits of capital punishment are illusory, but the bloodshed and the resulting destruction of community decency are real.[18]

Death penalty advocates deny the brutalization argument by pointing to countries with higher execution rates than the United States:

> A crime is an unlawful act, legal punishment is a lawful act. . . . There is no evidence for brutalization caused by the death penalty. The idea that legal killing will lead to imitation by illegal killing, or to any increase in violent crime, is unsubstantiated. And proponents do not explain why legal imprisonment does not lead to kidnappings, or why violent crime in Singapore and Saudi Arabia, both renowned for executions and physical punishments, is so infrequent.[19]

Opponents say the cost to morality is unbearably high if executions do not save innocent future victims, while supporters justify violence to evildoers because their studies show that the death penalty is a deterrent to possible killers.

Execution of Innocent People

According to the Death Penalty Information Center's Innocence List, 127 death row inmates have been exonerated since 1971. To be included among the 127, defendants must have been convicted and sentenced to death, and their convictions then overturned. Some were acquitted when they were retried, or all charges were dropped against them, or they were given an absolute pardon by the governor after new evidence was uncovered.[20] The average number of years a convict served before he was exonerated and released from prison was nine and a half, almost a decade.

How do these innocent people end up on death row? Cardozo Law School's Innocence Project cites these common causes:

eyewitness misidentifications, unreliable or limited science, false confessions, government misconduct, informants ("snitches") who make false claims to get out of jail early, and bad lawyers.[21] The Innocence Project has used the new forensic science capabilities of DNA identification to free 16 of the 127 exonerated prisoners.

Those numbers are significant to death penalty opponents. Even more frightening are the numbers who were not saved before their executions. According to Northwestern University's Bluhm Legal Clinic, it is probable that 39 innocent people have been put to death since 1976 in the United States.[22]

Death penalty proponents respond to the claims of innocence by denying that real proof of innocence has ever been obtained in these cases—an understandable situation, reply opponents, because once an execution takes place, all official investigation into the case is closed.

An Innocent Man Executed in Texas

The prosecution claimed that seventeen-year-old gang member Ruben Cantu and fifteen-year-old David Garza broke into an unfinished house in San Antonio and shot two construction workers with a rifle. One of the laborers, Juan Moreno, survived. Three times, Moreno refused to identify the picture of Ruben Cantu as one of his attackers.

Months later Cantu shot and injured an off-duty policeman who provoked him in a bar incident, and Moreno was brought in again and pressured to identify Cantu for the murder at the construction site. This time Moreno identified the defendant, but later he admitted to falsely identifying Cantu and said that the man who shot the rifle looked nothing like Cantu.

Without physical evidence, Cantu was convicted solely on the basis of Moreno's later recanted testimony. On August 24, 1993, Cantu was executed by lethal injection.

Garza, who has confessed since to involvement in the burglary and murder, has asserted that his accomplice was not Ruben Cantu.

Death penalty opponents believe that the death penalty is not a deterrent to those who would commit heinous crimes.

Many capital punishment advocates agree that it is probable that a very small number of technically innocent prisoners have indeed been executed, but that the benefits of capital punishment outweigh those few wrongful deaths. Ambulances save lives, but once in a very long while, an ambulance is involved in an accident and kills someone. The benefits to society of ambulances and the death penalty, proponents would say, far outstrip the damage that is so rarely inflicted.

Inconsistency of Death Sentences

Opponents of capital punishment denounce the unpredictable choices of judges and juries. They say that sometimes criminals who commit the most heinous acts can be appealing in the courtroom and thus receive imprisonment, while people who commit lesser crimes but are not sympathetic receive the death penalty. Statistics show that women are rarely sentenced to death, while African Americans in southern states are overrepresented on death row. Geography, politics, and quality of counsel also play unfair roles in punishments.

In the case of *Furman v. Georgia* (1972) the Supreme Court recognized a lack of uniformity in how death penalty defendants were sentenced. Justice Potter Stewart wrote for the majority that a random handful of defendants had been singled out for death, and it seemed that race played a part in the selection.

The dissenting justices in the *Furman* case argued that capital punishment had always been considered an appropriate punishment in the American legal tradition, and that the Constitution recognizes the death penalty in the Fourteenth Amendment, which refers to the taking of life (". . . nor shall any State deprive any person of life, liberty, or property, without due process of law").

The *Furman* case suspended capital punishment for four years, while states acted to correct the inconsistencies of sentencing. Many states ordered that capital cases be tried in two parts, the first to determine guilt and the second to impose punishment. Standards were written to guide the discretion of judges and juries. When the death penalty was brought before the Supreme Court again in 1976 in *Gregg v. Georgia*, the Court decided that most states had fixed the inconsistency problem and

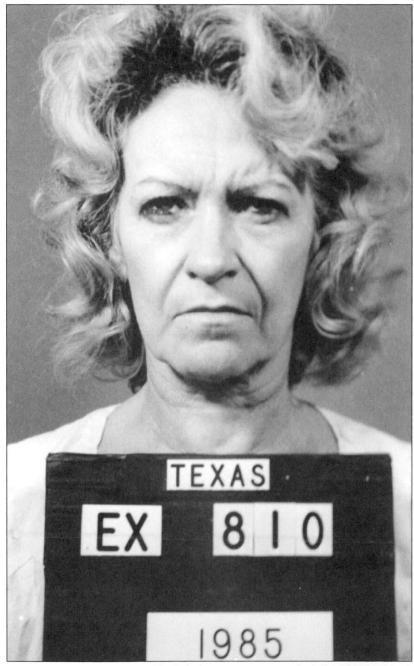

Betty Lou Beets was executed by lethal injection in 2000 for killing her husband in 1985. In general, however, women are less likely to be sentenced to death than men.

could execute defendants; states that had responded with statutes that ordered the death penalty automatically upon conviction in certain felonies had these statutes struck down.

Since 1976 opponents have cited inconsistencies that continue. Some states, regions, and counties are overrepresented in death penalty statistics; for instance, in 1999 only 9 percent of Ohio's murders occurred in Hamilton County (Cincinnati), but 25 percent of death sentences in Ohio came from Hamilton County.

Courts continue to spare the death penalty for women. Even though women are arrested for one in ten murders, they represent just one in fifty death sentences and only one in ninety-two executions.

EXECUTION OF INNOCENTS

"One thing is clear: no matter how hard we try, we cannot overcome the inevitable fallibility of being human. That fallibility means that we will not be able to apply the death penalty in a fair and just manner." —Russ Feingold, U.S. senator from Wisconsin.

Russ Feingold, statement on the Federal Death Penalty Abolition Act, November 16, 2000. www.senate.gov.

Defendants on death row are frequently defended by incapable lawyers. A Dallas newspaper investigation in 2000 revealed that one in four death row inmates was defended by a lawyer who was eventually disciplined, suspended, or banned from practicing law by the state bar. Supreme Court justice Ruth Bader Ginsburg said in 2001 that defendants with good lawyers do not get the death penalty; she added, "I have yet to see a death case among the dozens coming to the Supreme Court on eve-of-execution stay applications in which the defendant was well represented at trial."[23]

Execution of Juveniles

Death penalty opponents are particularly upset by the execution of minors. They believe that young people are not as responsible for their acts as adults are and that they may be rehabilitated as they grow into adulthood. Therefore, executions of young teenagers are often cited by opposition writers in their rationales.

In 1988 the Supreme Court case of *Thompson v. Oklahoma* held that execution of a prisoner who had committed his crime when he was aged fifteen or younger was cruel and unusual punishment, prohibited by the Eighth Amendment to the Constitution. Before the Thompson case, some states had no threshold age for executions at all.

In 1946 James Lewis Jr. and Charles Trudell, two fourteen-year-olds who worked in a Natchez, Mississippi, sawmill, robbed their boss and shot him in the course of the robbery. They confessed to the crime. In separate trials, they were each convicted and sentenced to death. The press and radio were drawn to the case because the boys were so young, and support poured in from around the country to stop the executions.

An attorney for Lewis and Trudell wrote in his local newspaper:

> It occurs to my mind that neither of the children is sufficiently large to fit into the various attachments of the electric chair. Therefore, I should like to respectfully suggest that we seat them as we do children at our dinner table, that we place books underneath them in order that their heads should be at the proper height to receive the death current; and I further urge that the books used for this purpose be the *Age of Reason, The Rise of Democracy in America*, a copy of the Constitution of the United States, and an appropriately bound edition of the Holy Bible. Then, with one current of electricity, the state of Mississippi can destroy all simultaneously.[24]

Despite national protests, electrocution instruments were adjusted to the children's measurements, and they were executed in 1947.

In *Stanford v. Kentucky* (1989) the Supreme Court held that the Eighth Amendment to the U.S. Constitution does not prohibit the death penalty for crimes committed at ages sixteen or seventeen. The sentence of Kevin Stanford, who had just turned seventeen when he committed the brutal rape and murder of a gas station attendant, was upheld. However, public opinion was turning against juvenile executions, and only three were held after 1989.

In 2005 the Court heard the case of *Roper v. Simmons* and held in a close five-to-four decision that the execution of offenders who were under the age of eighteen when their crimes were committed was unconstitutional. Christopher Simmons, an abused seventeen-year-old Missouri boy who took drugs, had planned and executed the murder of Mrs. Shirley Crook, whom he bound and threw into a river. His defense attorneys did not present evidence of his troubled youth or his drug abuse, but the crime was clearly premeditated and heinous. His appeal made it all the way to the Supreme Court; Roper, named in the case, was the director of the Missouri prison where Simmons sat on death row.

Legal briefs were submitted by medical and psychological organizations attesting to the difference between a teenage brain and an adult one, and to teenagers' incomplete faculties of reasoning and decision making. Dozens of Nobel Peace Prize

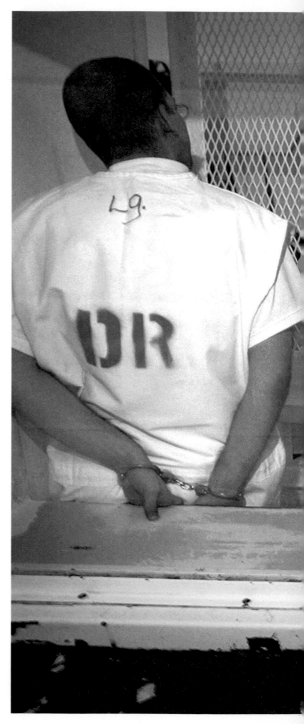

Texas inmate Leo Little (right) was seventeen when he committed a crime that led to his conviction and the death penalty. The U.S. Supreme Court, however, ruled in Roper v. Simmons *that the execution of offenders under the age of eighteen was unconstitutional.*

winners also wrote a brief urging the end of the death penalty for offenders who were not considered old enough to vote, serve in the military, or, in many states, to marry.

Justice Antonin Scalia wrote a dissenting opinion to the decision. He attacked the idea that public opinion had created a "national consensus" against execution of juveniles, since twenty of the thirty-eight states that had capital punishment on the books still allowed it for sixteen- and seventeen-year-olds. More important, Scalia argued that the important issue was not present-day consensus but rather whether execution of juveniles was considered cruel and unusual when the Bill of Rights was ratified.

He challenged the right of the Court to determine moral values and impose them on the people; this, he wrote, was the role of the elected legislature.

Retardation and Mental Illness

Opponents of the death penalty believe that the mentally deficient and the mentally ill are not in control of their acts and therefore cannot be punished for them in the same way that society punishes those who can think clearly and see the consequences of their choices. Especially in the case of mental retardation, the Court has limited the use of the death penalty.

In 1989 the Supreme Court dealt with diminished mental capacity in sentencing in the case of *Penry v. Lynaugh*. Penry, who raped and stabbed a woman to death, had a mental age of six and a half, although he was chronologically twenty-two years old. His IQ was that of a mild to moderately retarded individual. The Court decided that execution of mentally retarded individuals was not in violation of the Eighth Amendment against cruel and unusual punishments; mental retardation was instead just a mitigating factor to be considered by the judges and juries during sentencing.

The Court did strike down the execution of the mentally handicapped in 2002, in *Atkins v. Virginia*. Daryl Atkins had prior felony convictions; he and an accomplice had driven their victim to an automatic teller machine, and one of them shot the victim to death. Each of the defendants said the other had done the shooting, but the jury blamed Atkins. On appeal, the de-

Gas Chamber Execution of David Lawson

David Lawson, aged thirty-eight, was executed for the murder of Wayne Shinn, who had caught Lawson breaking into his house in 1980.

Sister Helen Prejean is a famous death penalty opponent. Her story has been told in the press and in the award-winning film *Dead Man Walking.* Prejean wrote about Lawson's execution:

> "David Lawson chose to die in the gas chamber. He said he wanted the people of North Carolina to know they were killing a man. In a last appeal to the U.S. Supreme Court, David Lawson's lawyers requested a stay of execution, arguing that execution by gas was a form of cruel punishment and in violation of the Eighth Amendment, but the Court refused to hear the petition.

It took thirteen minutes for the gas to kill him. . . . Soon after 2:00 A.M., the cyanide was dropped into the acid and the lethal fumes began to rise. Lawson, choking and gasping and straining against the straps, took short breaths and cried out, "I am a human. I am a human being." . . . Drool and tears slid from under the mask. A few deep breaths of the gas would have killed him sooner, but David Lawson continued to take short breaths and despite paroxysms of choking cried out until his voice was but a whisper: "I . . . am . . . a . . . human . . . being."

Sister Helen Prejean, *The Death of Innocents.* New York: Random House, 2005, pp. 264–65.

fense had Atkins evaluated by a psychologist, who found him to be mildly mentally retarded. The majority opinion by Justice John Paul Stevens argued that the main purposes of capital punishment, retribution and deterrence, would not be served by executing mentally retarded individuals. Such defendants could not be held as accountable for their actions as people of normal intelligence, wrote Stevens, and the death penalty had to be eliminated as punishment for them, although other consequences were appropriate.

Mental illness as a mitigating factor was decided in the Florida case of *Ford v. Wainwright* in 1986. Alvin Bernard Ford, convicted of murder and sent to death row in 1974, was clearly insane; he referred to himself as the pope, and said that he himself had appointed nine new justices to the Florida Supreme Court and that he was free to leave the prison any time he wanted. A panel of psychiatrists examined him and decided that Ford was psychotic but could still understand the nature of the death penalty. Ford sued Louie L. Wainwright, the director of the Florida Department of Corrections. The majority decision by Justice Thurgood Marshall asserted that the execution of the insane was "savage and inhuman" and did not serve any of the goals of capital punishment. The opinion also required adequate procedures for determining the mental competence of defendants.

Racial Discrimination

Opponents of the death penalty have conducted statistical studies over many years that show the color of the defendant frequently determines whether the death penalty is applied. Studies of capital punishment show that more death sentences and executions occur in the South than elsewhere in the United States, and that black convicts are overrepresented on death row and in actual executions.

In 1944 Gunnar Myrdal wrote *An American Dilemma: The Negro Problem and Modern Democracy*. This fifteen-hundred-page study was funded by the Carnegie Foundation, which chose a non-American to do the research because he could be unbiased. Myrdal found clear evidence that black Americans came in for much more than their share of the executions. He said this was due to a legacy of slavery, which prejudiced some southern juries against African Americans. Slaves had been considered dangerous and aggressive by their owners, who feared uprisings like Nat Turner's. This conception continued into the modern era to influence the minds of some people, particularly in the South. Between 1930 and the end of 1996, 4,220 prisoners were executed in the United States, and 53 percent of them were black.[25]

Studies in individual states confirm that race and geography play a role in death sentences. Even in federal capital cases, this

Family members mourn the death of Jonny Ray Conner on the day of his execution by lethal injection in August 2007.

is true: In 2000 the Justice Department reported that 80 percent of the 682 cases sent to the department for approval to seek the death penalty had minority defendants. Forty percent of the cases were filed in just five jurisdictions. Attorney general Janet Reno announced that she was sorely troubled by these statistics and ordered investigations of the racial and ethnic disparities.

Death penalty proponents point out that 50 percent of those arrested for murder in 1996 were black; of the thirty-two hundred prisoners on death row in that year, 40 percent were black. Proponents also select and propose their own statistics:

> Since 1929, white murderers have been more likely to have been executed than black murderers . . . white murderers, no matter who they kill, are more likely to get the death penalty than black murderers (11.1% to 7.3%). Furthermore, whites who kill whites are slightly more likely to be on death row than blacks who kill whites. Finally, whites who kill blacks are slightly more likely to be on death row than blacks who kill whites.[26]

The race of the victim also prejudices death row outcomes. The killing of a white person brings the defendant a death sentence markedly more often than the killing of a nonwhite. Professors at the University of North Carolina analyzed the records of 502 murder trials in that state between 1993 and 1997 and found that the race of the victim prejudiced the sentencing outcomes.

Professors Jack Boger and Isaac Unah of the University of North Carolina found that defendants whose victims are white are 3.5 times more likely to be sentenced to death than those whose victims were nonwhite. "The odds are supposed to be zero that race plays a role," said Dr. Unah. "No matter how the data was analyzed, the race of the victim always emerged as an important factor in who received the death penalty."[27]

Jury selection slants outcomes as well, the opponents claim. A prosecutor in Alabama disqualified several jurors because they were affiliated with Alabama State University, a predominantly black campus. Dobie Gillis Williams, whose story was told by prominent death penalty opponent Sister Helen Prejean, was tried by an all-white jury; the blacks in the jury panel were all struck from the jury by the prosecutor. Williams was executed in 1999.

THE FINANCIAL AND MORAL COSTS

"The death penalty exacts a terrible price in dollars, lives and human decency. Rather than tamping down the flames of violence, it fuels them." —Robert M. Morgenthau, district attorney, Manhattan.

Quoted in *Daily Record*, "It Is Time to Say 'Enough' to Death Penalty," December 20, 2004.

Racial slurs in courtrooms can go unnoticed or unpunished. The Florida Supreme Court upheld the sentence of a defendant whose white judge used such language in open court. In Missouri, Judge Earl Blackwell, who is white, was presiding over a murder case in which the defendant, Brian Kinder, was an unemployed black man. Blackwell told the press that he was changing political parties because he did not favor helping minorities: "The truth is that I have noticed in recent years that the Democrat party places far too much emphasis on representing minorities such as homosexuals, people who don't want to work, and people with a skin that's any color but white."[28] Kinder's lawyer made a motion to have the judge disqualify himself on the basis of prejudice, but it was denied.

Execution as Cruel and Unusual Punishment

Arguments that any form of execution constitutes cruel and unusual punishment stem from the Eighth Amendment to the Constitution, which reads: "Excessive bail shall not be required, nor excessive fines imposed, nor cruel and unusual punishments inflicted."

Execution is in and of itself cruel and unusual, opponents believe. They enumerate the horror stories of specific execution methods that cause slow and painful death. Supporters of the death penalty respond to the claims of cruel and unusual punishment by pointing out that the death row inmates' victims are

Summary of Opponents' Arguments

The death penalty is opposed for the following reasons:

1. *Brutalization.* The death penalty increases violence in society and turns all of us into accomplices to institutionalized murder.

2. *Execution of innocents.* Judges and juries have made mistakes, and the blood of innocent people is on everyone's hands.

3. *Inconsistency.* Some convicts are sentenced to die who have committed less horrible crimes than others whose lives are spared.

4. *Execution of juveniles.* Teenagers do not have adult judgment and control, mitigating factors that should spare their lives.

5. *Retardation and mental illness.* Mental incompetence must also be mitigating factors to spare defendants' lives.

6. *Racism.* Discrimination against minority defendants and in favor of white victims causes those defendants to be sentenced too often to death.

7. *Cruel and unusual punishment.* Execution is in and of itself cruel, and botched executions are a form of public torture.

human beings too. Most of the victims, they say, suffered much more painful deaths than those inflicted by lethal injection, the most common execution method in the United States today.

Since the case of Caryl Chessman, who was executed for a 1948 kidnapping in California, publishers and moviemakers have held a high profile in the anti–death penalty community. Chessman, who studied law in prison and wrote his own appeal briefs, authored four books about his plight. He was the subject of two Hollywood movies, the documentary *Justice and Caryl Chessman* (1960), and the feature film *Kill Me If You Can* (1977), in which Alan Alda played Chessman.[29]

THE ROAD TO THE DEATH PENALTY IN THE UNITED STATES

A series of twentieth-century Supreme Court cases culminated in a powerful challenge to capital punishment in the first decade of the twenty-first century. Many death penalty supporters feared that the 2007 case of *Baze v. Rees*, which the Court decided in 2008, would provide a clear opening for the Court to rule that all executions by lethal injection (and perhaps, by eventual extension, other methods) was a cruel and unusual punishment and thus unconstitutional, as death penalty opponents fervently hoped the Court would decide. However, the Court ruled in April 2008 in the *Baze* case that lethal injection executions do not violate the Eighth Amendment, and thus that they could continue throughout the United States.

Supreme Court decisions are an excellent barometer of policy and perception about the death penalty in the United States. The Court has generally ruled more and more to limit executions but remains steadfast in its desire to keep some form of capital punishment on the books. The rulings in particular cases over the last forty years show this pattern.

A case can make its way to the Supreme Court in three different ways. The first is an appeal based on facts from the original trial; the second is based on new evidence or lawyer problems. These appeals have to make their way through various levels of lower courts before the Supreme Court will consider hearing them. The third type of appeal is based on a possible violation of the Constitution, which must go directly into the federal court system. When the Supreme Court makes a decision in a case, it dictates policy for all fifty states. The cases from several states that are described in this chapter thus trace a long trail of decisions from local to national courtrooms.

Witherspoon v. Illinois, 1968

William G. Witherspoon was convicted of shooting a policeman to death in Chicago. Illinois law permitted the automatic exclusion of any juror in a potential death penalty case who was opposed to or had "conscientious scruples" against the death penalty. Witherspoon appealed the state court's guilty verdict on the basis of the bias of the jury. He claimed that those who accepted capital punishment would be more likely to find him guilty than the population at large.

In the majority decision, Justice Stewart wrote that the Court reversed Witherspoon's sentence because the systematic exclusion of jurors who were merely on the fence about capital punishment deprived him of an impartial hearing. The only jurors who could be excluded were those who said they would automatically vote against the death penalty in all cases.

Witherspoon v. Illinois was the first case that showed that the Supreme Court was willing to limit state practices in capital cases, and it opened the door to forty years of subsequent Supreme Court decisions on the death penalty.

Furman v. Georgia, 1972

The National Association for the Advancement of Colored People's Legal Defense Fund (LDF) mounted a campaign to bring the entire issue of capital punishment to the Supreme Court as a violation of the Eighth and Fourteenth Amendments to the Constitution. Four cases were grouped together to be heard by the Court under the title of just one of them, the *Furman* case.

The LDF argued that "evolving standards of decency" made the death penalty unacceptable, even though forty-one states had it on their books. The only reason this was so, LDF said, was that the enforcement of it was so rare; only a handful of poor, minority

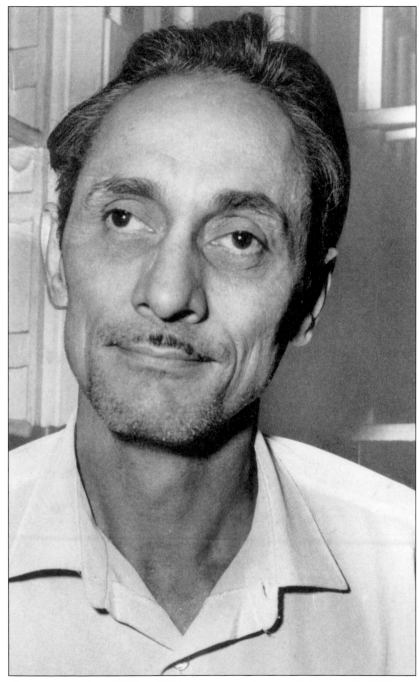

*Convicted murderer William Witherspoon was the central figure in the U.S.
Supreme Court case* Witherspoon v. Illinois.

convicts were ever put to death, and this was why the American public looked the other way. It was cruel and unusual punishment to single out this small group of people for a consequence that would be condemned if it were doled out evenhandedly and more widely.

Lawyers for the states protested that the Court did not have the role to make laws for the people, which only legislatures in the states could do. If the death penalty was applied in a biased way, the issue was equal protection under the laws under the Fourteenth Amendment and not the legality of capital punishment altogether. Furthermore, the small fraction of executions showed not prejudice but extreme care by judges and juries.

The justices of the Supreme Court did not issue the usual majority and minority decisions: Each justice authored his own. The decision was five to four to abolish capital punishment as practiced in the *Furman* cases, because it was cruel and unusual punishment under the Eighth Amendment. Each of the dissenting justices wrote an opinion agreeing with the defense

Elmer Branch, one of the plaintiffs in the 1972 Furman v. Georgia *case, shows the headline to another inmate after the Supreme Court decided that the death penalty constituted cruel and unusual punishment.*

that the issue was one for state legislatures, not for the Court, which was invading the power of those legislatures.

LETHAL INJECTION IS TORTURE

"Like electrocution or gassing, death by lethal injection is nothing more than the latest technological innovation of a practice that will never be humane, painless, rapid, or dignified." —Vittorio Bufacchi, professor of philosophy, and Laura Fairrie, documentary filmmaker.

Vittorio Bufacchi and Laura Fairrie, "Execution as Torture," *Peace Review*, vol. 13, 2001.

At the same time as the verdict was announced, the Court reversed the death sentences in one hundred capital cases under appeal. The decision suspended the capital punishment laws of the United States as they were written at the time and saved the lives of sixty-three inmates facing execution around the country.

Conservatives around the country, led by President Richard Nixon, strongly opposed the *Furman* verdict. They worked to reinstate the death penalty by fixing inconsistencies in state sentencing laws and providing clearer guidelines for judges and juries to follow in capital cases.

Gregg v. Georgia, 1976

This Georgia case was the result of efforts to reform death penalty statutes in the states and reinstate capital punishment, and these efforts were successful. The Court ruled that the new death penalty statutes in Florida, Georgia, and Texas fulfilled the requirements set out in *Furman* for objectivity in sentencing. Inmates sentenced under such laws could be executed, wrote the majority. Executions resumed in 1977.

Woodson v. North Carolina, 1976

Furman v. Georgia had struck down the death penalty because of the wide latitude some states afforded in capital cases for juries and judges to send defendants to death row. North Carolina responded to this critique by removing the jurists' power altogether and prescribing the death penalty for every first-degree murder conviction. In *Woodson v. North Carolina* the Supreme Court found this equally unacceptable. The justices decided that North Carolina was not granting *enough* latitude to consider mitigating factors. The Court was narrowing carefully the use of the death penalty it had restored under *Gregg*.

McCleskey v. Kemp, 1987

The NAACP Legal Defense Fund brought the case of Warren McCleskey, a black man convicted of killing a white Atlanta police officer and sentenced to death in the electric chair by eleven white jurors and only one black juror. The LDF based its case on a study of Georgia death penalty cases by David Baldus, a professor at the University of Iowa. The Baldus study analyzed two thousand murder cases in Georgia and showed that black defendants received the death penalty markedly more often than white defendants; the difference was even more striking when comparing death penalty sentences for black defendants who killed white victims to sentences for white defendants who killed black victims.

In the opinion of the Court in the case of *McCleskey v. Kemp*, Justice Lewis Powell reviews the study:

> The Baldus study is actually two sophisticated statistical studies that examine over 2,000 murder cases that occurred in Georgia during the 1970s. The raw numbers collected by Professor Baldus indicate that defendants charged with killing white persons received the death penalty in 11% of the cases, but defendants charged with killing blacks received the death penalty in only 1% of the cases. The raw numbers also indicate a reverse racial disparity according to the race of the defendant: 4% of the black defendants received the death penalty, as opposed to 7% of the white defendants.[30]

The Legal Defense Fund claimed that capital punishment was not doled out with an even hand in Georgia, violating the Fourteenth

Mitigating Factors: Sandra Lockett's Case

Sandra Lockett was a recovering heroin addict from Akron, Ohio, with a minor criminal record. When she was twenty-one she visited New Jersey with her friend Joanne Baxter. While there, the women met Al Parker and Nathan Earl Dew. Parker and Dew came back with the girls to their home in Akron without the money to buy transportation back to New Jersey. Dew offered to pawn his ring, but the group's thoughts turned instead to robbing a pawnshop with a gun Sandra's father kept in his basement.

Sandra knew the owner of the pawn shop personally, so she waited in the getaway car when the others attempted the robbery. Al Parker held the gun, which went off and killed the pawnbroker. Sandra hid the gun when she heard what had happened. Eventually all of the participants were apprehended and charged with murder.

To avoid the death penalty, Parker—who had his hand on the trigger—took a plea bargain so that he would testify against the others. Lockett was also offered a plea bargain, and she turned it down three times.

The jury was instructed that "if the conspired robbery and the manner of its accomplishment would be reasonably likely to produce death, each plotter is equally guilty." Lockett was convicted. The state of Ohio limited the "mitigating circumstances" her lawyer could present at sentencing, and Sandra's heroin addiction, her relatively minor criminal record, and her dismay at the unexpected death of the pawnbroker could not be considered.

The Supreme Court reversed her sentence, and in its decision eliminated any limitations on testimony that can be introduced as mitigating the circumstances of a capital crime.

Justia.com: US Supreme Court Center. http://supreme .justia.com/us/438/586/case.html.

Amendment's guarantee of equal protection of the laws. An outcome for the defense could overturn capital punishment altogether, as tainted by racism.

The Supreme Court's five-to-four majority decision against McCleskey was written by Justice Powell, who found that in Mc-Cleskey's individual case, no specific bias of the jury had been shown, even though the general difference between the treatment of black and white defendants was established in the Baldus report. The decision was considered a major victory for death penalty proponents and a serious blow to death penalty abolitionists.

Thompson v. Oklahoma, 1988

William Wayne Thompson, a fifteen-year-old boy, participated in his brother-in-law's murder in Oklahoma. He could be tried as an adult under Oklahoma law if the court decided that the crime justified it. He was convicted as an adult and sentenced to death. He appealed on the grounds that executing him for a crime he committed as a minor would constitute cruel and unusual punishment.

Death row inmate William Wayne Thompson (center) committed murder in Oklahoma when he was fifteen years old. He was convicted and sentenced to death, but in 1988 the U.S. Supreme Court reversed the sentence.

In a five-to-four opinion, the Supreme Court reversed the sentence, coming just short of declaring that no one under sixteen could be executed. In effect, the Thompson case ended the execution of anyone under the age of sixteen. In 2004 the case of *Roper v. Simmons* extended the protection of juveniles from the death penalty to all who were under the age of eighteen at the time the crime was committed.

Penry v. Lynaugh, 1989

John Paul Penry, arrested for the rape and murder of a woman in Texas, had a competency hearing before his trial that revealed that he was mentally retarded, with the mental abilities of a six-and-a-half-year-old child. A psychologist described his social abilities as that of a nine- or ten-year-old. Despite these findings, the jury at that hearing found him competent to stand trial.

DEATH BY LETHAL INJECTION IS PAINLESS

"Sodium pentothal is given to an inmate first to render him completely unconscious and insensible to pain. . . . The inmate receives 3 grams, or 10 times the normal amount based on body weight. I can attest with all medical certainty that anyone receiving that massive dose will be under anesthesia." —Kyle Janek, Texas state senator and anesthesiologist.

Kyle Janek, "Attack on Texas' Legal Injections Is Bogus," February 1, 2004. www.prodeath penalty.org.

During the trial Penry's lawyers claimed that he was incapable of learning and could not distinguish right from wrong. The prosecution introduced testimony from experts who said that Penry did know right from wrong but had an antisocial personality disorder. The jury sided with the prosecution and convicted him of murder, and during the penalty phase of the trial he was sentenced to death.

The laws in Texas did not provide for the central role of Penry's mental retardation as a mitigating factor in his sentencing.

Penry's lawyers brought this up on appeal, along with the claim that execution of the mentally retarded would constitute cruel and unusual punishment.

The Supreme Court overturned Penry's conviction and instructed the state of Texas to change its sentencing procedures so that mental retardation would be given full weight as a mitigating factor. However, the Court refused to bar execution categorically for the mentally retarded, noting that the abilities of retarded people vary greatly, and each case must be examined separately.

In 2002 this decision was reversed in *Atkins v. Virginia*, when the Supreme Court disallowed executions of the mentally deficient. Atkins, who had an IQ of fifty-nine, had never lived on his own or held a job. The decision in this case was written by Justice Stevens: "We are not persuaded that the execution of mentally retarded criminals will measurably advance the deterrent or the retributive purpose of the death penalty."[31]

Payne v. Tennessee, 1991

Pervis Tyrone Payne was accused of attacking a twenty-eight-year-old mother of two young children. The woman and one of the children died. One child survived the attack. The prosecution presented a "victim impact statement" describing the pain and suffering of the surviving child. The defendant appealed on the grounds that this kind of statement was "prejudicial" and violated the defendant's rights. Former cases had banned victim impact testimony, but this time the Supreme Court affirmed its legality. This decision was seen as part of the growth of a victims' rights movement throughout the United States and as support for the pro–death penalty cause.

Herrera v. Collins, 1993

Leonel Herrera was convicted of killing two police officers in Texas. Two eyewitnesses, one a victim who subsequently died, testified that Herrera was the murderer. Herrera received the death penalty and began a series of appeals, the first of which claimed that the eyewitnesses were unreliable. This appeal was turned down by the Texas Court of Appeals, and the Supreme Court refused to review the case.

The Victims' Rights Movement

In recent years the public has become more aware of the suffering caused by crime, especially murder, through television shows hosted by John Walsh (*America's Most Wanted*), Nancy Grace, and others. Walsh's son and Grace's fiancé were murder victims.

The victims' rights movement seeks to ensure the rights of victims' families to be present and to be heard in all legal proceedings of the case, including plea bargaining and parole hearings, and to be notified if the criminal escapes from prison. It also calls for financial benefits and human services to be given by the government to victims. Most significantly for the death penalty issue, victims' rights advocates call for tougher sentences for criminals and for increasing the use of the death penalty in murder cases.

Supporters of victims' rights legislation cross political parties and philosophies. On January 7, 2003, liberal California senator Dianne Feinstein joined conservative Arizona senator Jon Kyl to propose a Victims' Rights Amendment to the Constitution. Its centerpiece statement reads:

> A victim of violent crime shall have the right to reasonable and timely notice of any public proceeding involving the crime and of any release or escape of the accused; the rights not to be excluded from such public proceeding and reasonably to be heard at public release, plea, sentencing, reprieve, and pardon proceedings; and the right to adjudicative decisions that duly consider the victim's safety, interest in avoiding unreasonable delay, and just and timely claims to restitution from the offender.

National Victims' Constitutional Amendment Passage. www.nvcap.org.

John Walsh, host of the Fox television show America's Most Wanted, *is a leading advocate of the victims' rights movement.*

Herrera's next appeal came much later. He claimed that his own brother told Herrera's lawyer and son that he, not Herrera, had pulled the trigger and killed the policemen. However, Herrera's brother died before the appeal was filed. The Texas appeals court threw out the case, because during the original trial this evidence had not been introduced.

Herrera then appealed to the Supreme Court. The Court had to consider whether the federal courts were obligated to hear appeals in death row cases on the basis of innocence, even if the grounds of innocence appear many years after the trial. By a six-to-three decision, the Supreme Court decided against Herrera, noting that his witnesses were no longer around to be cross-examined. The issue of the lapse of time was critical. The Court was saying that appeals like Herrera's could go on forever, and at some point, legal closure is necessary.

Ring v. Arizona, 2002

Timothy Ring and two accomplices robbed an armored car of $562,000 in cash and shot the driver to death. Under Arizona's felony murder law, the jury convicted Ring of first-degree murder, but the full evidence necessary to sentence him to death was not presented at the jury trial. At the sentencing hearing, Ring's partners testified against him, and the judge found that enough aggravating factors (especially the elaborate planning of the robbery and the cruel and depraved manner of the murder) applied to Ring's crime and qualified him for the death penalty.

The main issue in the Ring case was whether a jury, not simply the judge, should decide a death sentence. The majority opinion, written by Justice Ginsburg, declared that the jury's deliberation was required and overturned Ring's sentence.

Baze v. Rees, 2008

Two inmates of Kentucky's death row, Ralph Baze and Thomas Bowling, appealed their death sentences on the grounds that lethal injection, the method of execution in the majority of American states, would violate the Eighth Amendment's prohibition of cruel and unusual punishment. Theirs was one of many cases that appealed on the same grounds, but it was the one granted a Supreme Court hearing.

As soon as certiorari (a hearing by the Supreme Court) was announced on September 26, 2007, executions were halted across the United States. The Supreme Court hears death penalty cases all the time, but this was the first case the Court had considered concerning the *method* of execution since *Wilkerson v. Utah* in 1879, when it decided that executions by firing squad did not constitute cruel and unusual punishment.

Death by lethal injection involves the intravenous injection of three drugs, a lethal cocktail. The first drug is an anesthetic to put the convict to sleep; the second causes complete paralysis; the third brings about cardiac arrest. The possibility exists that the prisoner could regain consciousness during the final stage, and the effect of the third injection, cardiac arrest, would certainly cause great suffering.

This has happened in some instances, partly because trained physicians cannot carry out executions due to their professional ethics, and prison technicians have botched executions, causing extended and excruciating deaths. Nine states recognized these problems in the year before the *Baze* case and stopped their executions until a better method was found.

The Court heard oral arguments on January 7, 2008, and handed down its ruling on April 16. Seven justices rejected the challenge to lethal injection. Only two, Justices Ginsburg and David Souter, disagreed.

On the evening of May 6, 2008, the state of Georgia executed killer William Earl Lynd, the first execution since the *Baze* decision was handed down. Lynd had killed his girlfriend and kidnapped and shot another woman to death while fleeing the scene of the murder. One hour before the execution, the Supreme Court denied a stay of execution. Lynd declined any final words, and seventeen minutes after injections were administered he was pronounced dead. At the state capitol in Atlanta that night, a small group of protesters held a banner that read, "Stop the Death Penalty."

The Supreme Court continues to hear and rule on death penalty cases. On April 16, 2008, the justices heard arguments in *Kennedy v. Louisiana*. Patrick Kennedy was convicted of raping his eight-year-old stepdaughter and was sentenced to die. Louisiana is the only state that allows the death penalty for anything short of

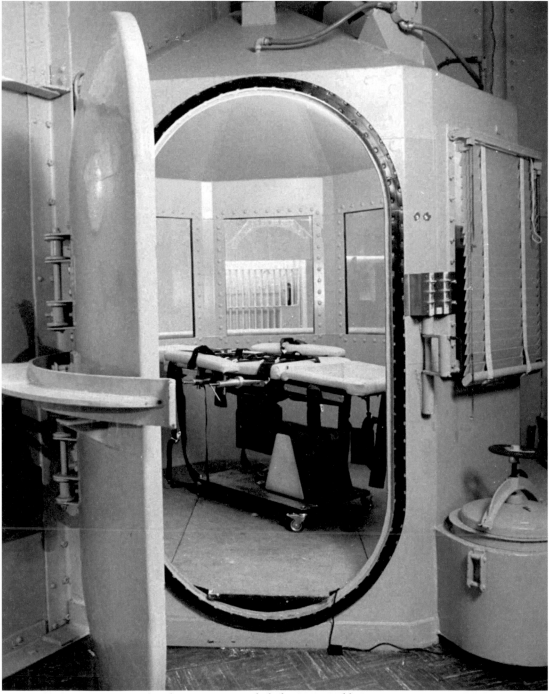

An execution chamber containing a lethal injection table.

murder; one other inmate is on Louisiana's death row for rape of a child, but no one has been executed in the United States for anything but murder since 1962. Kennedy's lawyers argued that applying the death penalty in crimes that did not result in the death of the victim is cruel and unusual punishment. The Court agreed on June 25, 2008, that a state may not impose the death penalty against an individual for committing a crime that did not result in the death of the victim.

CHAPTER 5

THE DEATH PENALTY AROUND THE GLOBE

According to Amnesty International, in 2007 twenty-four of the world's countries executed 1,252 individuals; the greatest number of executions were carried out in China (470 deaths), Iran (317), Saudi Arabia (143), Pakistan (135), Iraq (65), and the United States (43). Over 3,000 people were sentenced to death in fifty-one countries, and more than 20,000 convicts live on death row around the globe. However, the majority of nations have outlawed capital punishment.[32]

Number One: China

China leads all other countries in use of the death penalty. On April 8 the Olympic torch made its way through Paris on its way to the 2008 Olympic Games in Beijing, China. Demonstrators from the group *Coalition mondiale contre la peine de mort* ("World coalition against the death penalty") used the event to protest in the Paris city hall square against China's executions. They were joined by Belgian protesters and other Europeans against capital punishment. Death penalty advocates, along with opponents, have criticized the Chinese for the excessive and arbitrary nature of capital punishment in China. The Chinese have responded that executions have diminished greatly in number in the past few years.

Executions in China: 2001–2008

Amnesty International reported in 2001 that China executed 1,781 people in three months of that year. This was more than the rest of the world combined executed in three years. The death penalty was doled out to those convicted not only of murder or

other violent crimes but also of offenses like bribery, tax fraud, drug trafficking, selling harmful foodstuffs, and even stealing gasoline.

Some of the executions were blamed on an aggressive anticrime campaign called "Strike Hard." In Hunan Province, police claimed to have solved three thousand cases in just two days in April. In Sichuan Province, the police said they arrested almost twenty thousand people in six days. Most executions took place after "sentencing rallies" in public sports arenas and venues filled with spectators. On the way to the firing squads that would execute them, the convicts were paraded through the streets.

China continues to execute criminals by firing squads using assault rifles, but it has begun to also use lethal injection; in fact, protesters claim that lethal injection has been used more frequently to kill high officials, while ordinary people still face the firing squad.

The world's protests against capital punishment in China berate the country for the swift imposition of the death penalty, usually less than a year after sentencing, giving the prisoner little chance for appeal. Also, the imposition of the death penalty is uneven

China uses the death penalty more than any country in the world. Here, police officers pretend to shoot prisoners during a practice execution drill.

Trial of a Tyrant

The execution of Saddam Hussein by hanging occurred at dawn on the morning of December 30, 2006. The dictator had received an extended and tortuous trial, which ended in conviction for his role in the 1982 massacre of 148 Iraqis who were accused of plotting an assassination attempt against him. The White House statement by President George W. Bush said, "Fair trials were unimaginable under Saddam Hussein's tyrannical rule. It is a testament to the Iraqi people's resolve to move forward after decades of oppression that, despite his terrible crimes against his own people, Saddam Hussein received a fair trial."

Quoted in CNN.com, "Hussein Executed with 'Fear in His Face,'" December 30, 2006. www.cnn.com/2006/WORLD/meast/12/29/hussein/index.html.

and unfair: When "Strike Hard" campaigns are staged by the central government, local officials respond with rapid trials and wholesale executions.[33]

Number Two: Iran

Capital offenses in Iran include murder, terrorism, drug-related offenses, and sexual crimes such as child sexual abuse and rape. Adultery is also a capital crime. Drug trafficking represents a high proportion of these offenses. Occasionally the executions are carried out in public, and they are usually by hanging. Sex offenses may attract death by stoning, as in the recent case of the Kabiri sisters.

In February 2008 Amnesty International reported that two Iranian women, Zohreh Kabiri, twenty-seven years old, and Azar Kabiri, twenty-eight, were arrested and convicted of adultery. Branch Eighty of the Karaj Penal Court of Tehran Province sentenced the women to death by stoning. Iran's supreme court upheld the ruling.

The Manchester *Guardian* reported the international community's reaction to Iran's method of capital punishment:

> Iran was urged today to abolish immediately executions by stoning, described by Amnesty International as a "grotesque and horrific" form of punishment.

An Iranian woman dresses up as a victim of stoning during a demonstration.
Human rights group Amnesty International has called on Iran to abolish
executions by stoning.

The head of Iran's judiciary imposed a moratorium on such executions in 2002, but two people were stoned to death in 2006 and one last year [2007], Amnesty said. Nine women and two men are currently under sentence of death by stoning.

Amnesty said in a new report that article 204 of Iran's penal code "dictates that the stones are large enough to cause pain, but not so large as to kill the victim immediately."

The rules prescribe that men should be buried up to their waists and women up to their breasts for the purposes of death by stoning. Victims typically take 20 minutes to die.[34]

Number Three: Saudi Arabia

Offenses that can result in beheading in Saudi Arabia include witchcraft, adultery, homosexuality, and renouncing of Islam. About half of the executions in Saudi Arabia in 2007, seventy-six of them, involved foreigners.

A well-known case involved Rizana Nafeek, a seventeen-year-old servant from Sri Lanka who worked in Saudi Arabia with forged documents. While under her care, the baby in the household she served died. According to Nafeek, as she fed the infant boy on May 22, 2005, he started to choke; she shouted for help

Nearly half of the executions in Saudi Arabia involve foreigners. Here, the father of Rizana Nafeek of Sri Lanka, who was on death row for allegedly murdering an infant boy in a household in which she was a servant, holds up a newspaper story about his daughter.

while attempting to clear the baby's airway. The mother ran in, but by that time the infant was unconscious or dead.

The family had Nafeek arrested, accusing her of strangling their son to death. She signed a police confession that she later withdrew, when it was ultimately translated for her. Nafeek, along with most foreign nationals in Saudi Arabia, have insufficient legal representation and, following interrogations without interpreters, sign documents written in Arabic, which they cannot read.

If her sentence is confirmed by the central court in Riyadh, the young Sri Lankan maid will be beheaded by sword in public. The worldwide outcry and collecting of petitions has so far stayed her execution.

Number Four: Pakistan

Over seven thousand convicts are on death row in Pakistan, where executions are commonly performed by hanging. The death sentence may be imposed for twenty-seven different charges. These include the capital crimes commonly punished elsewhere, such as murder or rape, and also blasphemy, stripping a woman of her clothes in public, and sabotage of the railway system.

The *Daily Times* of Pakistan, which names itself "a new voice for a new Pakistan," wrote on its editorial page in January 2007: "We have retained the death penalty, with a lot of other countries in the world, because we think it will deter the killers among us. . . . But the record shows that death is no deterrence. The big hangings in Pakistan as elsewhere have actually aroused conflicting passions and negated the concept of deterrence."[35]

The Federally Administered Tribal Areas of Pakistan that border Afghanistan have experienced an increase in unlawful executions, called honor killings, among supporters of the ultraconservative Taliban. Honor killings punish crimes that are said to bring shame upon a family. In conservative societies, honor crimes can consist of such infractions as marriage without the parents' consent; in one extreme case, a man murdered his wife and daughters for leaving the home without permission. These honor killings have increased in the tribal areas, and they are strictly condemned by human rights organizations in the country, as well as by the Pakistani government, which prosecutes the perpetrators when it can find them.

Number Five: Iraq

For almost twenty-five years, Saddam Hussein's government (1979–2003) in Iraq executed its enemies at will, along with common criminals. There were 114 crimes that could be punished by death. The accused often had no trials at all, or hasty trials in which they were given no adequate representation. No totals are available, but Amnesty International documented more than eight hundred executions in just three years, 1980–1983. Many victims were nonviolent political prisoners who were members of banned political parties, students, and even children. Sometimes corpses were returned to their families for burial bearing evidence of torture.

A SMALL PERCENTAGE OF COUNTRIES, A LARGE PERCENTAGE OF EXECUTIONS

"Just five countries—China, Iran, Saudi Arabia, Pakistan and the USA—carried out the overwhelming majority (88%) of known executions in the world last year." —Amnesty International.

Quoted in Death Penalty Information Center, "The Death Penalty: An International Perspective." www.deathpenaltyinfo.org/death-penalty-international-perspective.

Following the American invasion of Iraq, U.S. administrator Paul Bremer suspended the death penalty to assure Iraqis that the terror of Saddam's regime was over. Iraqis felt that capital punishment was one of many ways that Saddam's regime had oppressed them, but the death penalty was reinstated in May 2005 in an attempt to restore order to revolutionary chaos in the country.

The law now includes some protection of the rights of the accused: Anyone sentenced to death receives an automatic appeal. However, executions are required within thirty days when all legal avenues are exhausted. In September 2005 three insurgents who had murdered and mangled their victims were executed, and a year later the Iraqi government hanged twenty-six men and one woman as insurgents committing "high crimes against civilians."[36]

Norwegian State Secretary Elisabeth Walaas's Address, October 10, 2007

"Globally, we have witnessed a decline in the use of the death penalty and a huge rise in the number of countries that have abolished this abhorrent practice in the last 10 years. However, a number of countries still carry out executions and some of them are even practising this form of punishment more often.

"Norway is a staunch defender of human rights, the dignity of the individual and the principle of humanity.

"Norway is fundamentally opposed to the use of death penalty, since it is wholly inconsistent with these principles. We believe that worldwide abolition of capital punishment will enhance human dignity and affirm respect for life. . . .

"The Rwandan people have suffered unspeakable crimes. And yet this very people showed wisdom and courage in deciding to abolish the death penalty earlier this year. Few things challenge our notions of justice and punishment more than coming to terms with the genocide in Rwanda. And yet now that Rwanda is rebuilding its society, it is doing so within the ambit of a death penalty–free zone.

"What a country with Rwanda's history can do, any country can do. . . . For 10 years now, Europe has been a de facto death penalty–free zone. The Council of Europe has been a pioneer in the abolition process, and promoted Europe as a role model in the global fight against capital punishment. The Council is therefore well placed to take on a further leadership role, and provide inspiration and sound arguments for future action.

"The next step in this process should be the establishment of a world-wide moratorium on the death penalty with a view to achieving its universal abolition."

Elisabeth Walaas, "Europe Against the Death Penalty," address at the First European Day Against the Death Penalty Conference, Lisbon, October 10, 2007. www.regjeringen.no/en/dep/ud/about_mfa/Other-political-staff/elisabeth_walaas/Speeches-and-articles/2007/.

Most Iraqis welcomed the return of capital punishment. The three murderers tried in 2005 were members of the Ansa al-Sunna Army. As the judge prepared to sentence them, he asked the victims' families for statements. "They broke his arms. They broke his legs. They took out his eyeballs," one woman said at the hearing, describing what the men had done to her son. "Death penalty. I want the death penalty."[37]

Singapore: Death Penalty Lowers Crime

The city-state of Singapore has 4 million people and one of the lowest crime rates in the world. The people and the lawmakers believe that the exemplary law and order apparent in their city is reason enough to continue capital punishment and that it must be a deterrent to criminal behavior.

SINGAPORE DEFENDS EXECUTIONS

"In criminal law legislation, our priority is the security and well being of law-abiding citizens rather than the rights of the criminal to be protected from incriminating evidence." —Lee Kuan Yew, Singapore's senior minister.

Quoted in Amy Tan, "Singapore Death Penalty Shrouded in Silence," Reuters News Service, April 12, 2002. www.singaporewindow.org/sw02/020412re.htm.

Capital punishment in Singapore is typically carried out before dawn on Friday mornings, and the state is secretive about executions. Statistics emerge slowly; the government revealed under questioning by its parliament in 2002 that 340 people were hanged, mainly for drug crimes, between 1991 and 2000. The secrecy prevents public appeals against the death penalty. Julia Suzanne Bohl, a twenty-three-year-old German citizen, however, had her sentence for carrying slightly more than five hundred grams of marijuana commuted from death to life imprisonment in 2002. Death penalty opponents in Singapore claim that the reason the issue is not debated publicly is that the education system and the press do not discuss capital punishment.

Algeria: A Retentionist African Nation

The continent using capital punishment the most is Africa. Many African nations have experienced political unrest during the past decades. The nation of Algeria is an example of a country that retains the death penalty to deter terrorism and revolution.

In 2008 Algeria had a criminal code that permitted capital punishment for many crimes. Most of the sentences were for terrorism charges, such as massacres, sabotage, or participation in armed bands, with a small number of sentences for murder and drug-related crimes.

Algeria's civil war of seven years ended with the election of Abdelaziz Bouteflika as president in 1999. As calm and order was restored into the twenty-first century, the country moved toward renouncing capital punishment for many crimes. In 2003 only fourteen death sentences were handed out in Algeria, and on December 18, 2007, Algeria voted in the UN General Assembly in favor of the United Nations Moratorium on the Use of the Death Penalty.

Despite the UN vote, several Algerian defendants have been sentenced to death in 2008 for murder and drug smuggling, and most often for membership in armed terrorist groups. Sometimes the terrorists are convicted in absentia, as the government attempts to suppress violent right-wing Islamist brigades.

The European Union: Abolitionist on the Death Penalty

The European Union (EU) requires its member nations to abolish the death penalty, and the EU has established October 10 each year as the European Day Against the Death Penalty. On the first of these commemorations, October 10, 2007, the EU sponsored a conference in Lisbon on the issue. Here, Norwegian state secretary Elisabeth Walaas spoke about the world's view of capital punishment. She lauded the nation of Rwanda, which had suffered a civil war even harsher than Algeria's, for its abolition of the death penalty.

The world's nations continue to be split on the issue of capital punishment. For some governments it is an outdated and inhumane practice, no matter the methods and no matter the rationale. Others, however, remain steadfast in their belief that capital punishment is a fair and reasonable way to punish criminals, deter crime, and protect society. Far from resolving itself,

Members of the South India Cell for Human Rights Education and Monitoring (SICHREM) hold placards and candles during an anti–death penalty rally on October 10, 2005. That day has been set aside each year by the European Union as European Day Against the Death Penalty.

this ancient debate just seems to get more complex as human civilizations evolve, grow, and continually redefine their moral and legal expectations.

Introduction: A Four-Thousand-Year-Old Debate

1. L.W. King, translator. *Exploring Ancient World Cultures: An Introduction to Ancient World Cultures on the World-Wide Web.* "Near East: Hammurabi's Code of Laws." http://eawc.evansville.edu/anthology/hammurabi.htm.
2. Cesare Beccaria, "Of the Punishment of Death," chap. 28, in *On Crimes and Punishments* (originally published in Italian, 1764). Philadelphia: R. Bell, 1778. www.constitution.org/cb/crim_pun.htm.

Chapter 1: The History of the Death Penalty

3. Leviticus 24:17–20.
4. Quoted in William B. Thayer, "Leges Corneliae," Bill Thayer's Web Site, December 23, 2006. http://penelope.uchicago.edu/Thayer/E/Roman/Texts/secondary/SMIGRA*/Leges_Corneliae.html.
5. Quoted in Marcus Tanner, "Henry the VIII: Henry the Horrible," *Independent* (London), October 12, 2003. http://findarticles.com/p/articles/mi_qn4159/is_200310/ai_n12746891.
6. Cesare Beccaria, "Of the Punishment of Death." www.constitution.org/cb/crim_pun.htm.
7. Quoted in PBS, "The Execution," *Frontline*, 1995.
8. Quoted in *New York Times*, "Iran: Amnesty Demands End to Stoning," January 16, 2008. http://query.nytimes.com/gst/fullpage.html?res=9C07E5DE1E3BF935A25752C0A96E9C8B63&&scp=1&sq=Iran:%20Amnesty%20Demands%20End%20to%20Stoning&st=cse.
9. ABC News, International Communications Research Poll, June 20, 2007.

Chapter 2: Arguments for the Death Penalty

10. Pew Forum on Religion and Public Life, *An Enduring Major-*

ity: Americans Continue to Support the Death Penalty, Pew Research Center, December 19, 2007. www.pewresearch.org.

11. Hashem Dezhbakhsh and Joanna M. Shepherd, "The Deterrent Effect of Capital Punishment: Evidence from a 'Judicial Experiment.'" *Economic Enquiry*, July 2006, pp. 512–35.

12. Dale O. Cloninger and Roberto Marchesini, "Execution Moratoriums, Commutations and Deterrence: The Case of Illinois." *Applied Economics*, May 20, 2006, pp. 967–73.

13. Death Penalty Information Center, "Facts About the Death Penalty," January 30, 2009. www.deathpenaltyinfo.org.

14. Ronald Radosh and Joyce Milton, *The Rosenberg File: A Search for the Truth*. New Haven, CT: Yale University Press, 1982, p. xiv.

15. Quoted in Gary P. Gershman, *Death Penalty on Trial*. Santa Barbara, CA: ABC-CLIO, 2005, p. 3.

16. American Civil Liberties Union, "The Case Against the Death Penalty," December 31, 1997. www.aclu.org/capital/general/10441pub19971231.html.

17. Philip J. Cook and Donna B. Slawson, *The Costs of Processing Murder Cases in North Carolina*. Durham, NC: Terry Sanford Institute of Public Policy, Duke University, 1993.

Chapter 3: Objections to the Death Penalty

18. American Civil Liberties Union, "The Case Against the Death Penalty."

19. Ernest van den Haag, "Capital Punishment Saves Innocent Lives," in *Does Capital Punishment Deter Crime?* Roman Espejo, ed. Detroit, MI: Thomson Gale, 2003, p. 27.

20. Death Penalty Information Center, "The Innocence List." http://deathpenaltyinfo.org/article.php?scid-6&did-110.

21. Innocence Project, "The Causes of Wrongful Convictions," Cardozo Law School. www.innocenceproject.org/understand.

22. Northwestern University, Bluhm Law Clinic Center on Wrongful Convictions, "Executing the Innocent." www.law.northwestern.edu/wrongfulconvictions/issues/death penalty/executinginnocent.

23. Quoted in Death Penalty Information Center, "Arbitrariness: Representation." http://deathpenaltyinfo.org/article.php?did=1328#Representation.

24. Quoted in Elaine Landau, *Teens and the Death Penalty*. Berkeley Heights, NJ: Enslow, 1992, pp. 47–48.
25. American Civil Liberties Union, "The Case Against the Death Penalty."
26. Jared Taylor, *Paved with Good Intentions*. New York: Carroll and Graf, 1992, pp. 40–41.
27. Quoted in Death Penalty Information Center, "Race and the Death Penalty." www.deathpenaltyinfo.org/race-and-death-penalty.
28. Quoted in *Kinder v. Bowersox*, 272 F. 3rd 532 (8th Cir. 2001). http://bulk.resource.org/courts.gov/c/F3/272/272.F3d.532.00-2807.html.
29. Robert M. Baird and Stuart Rosenbaum, *Punishment and the Death Penalty*. Amherst, NY: Prometheus, 1995, p. 121.

Chapter 4: The Road to the Death Penalty in the United States

30. Lewis Powell, opinion of the Court, *McCleskey v. Kemp*, 481 U.S. 279 (1987). www.law.cornell.edu/supct/html/historics/USSC_CR_0481_0279_ZO.html.
31. Quoted in The Oyez Project, "*Atkins v. Virginia*, 536 U.S. 304 (2002)." www.oyez.org/cases/2000-2009/2001/2001_00_8452/.

Chapter 5: The Death Penalty Around the Globe

32. Amnesty International, "Death Penalty: Death Sentences and Executions in 2007." www.amnesty.org/en/death-penalty/death-sentences-and-executions-in-2007.
33. BBC News World Service, "China 'Outstrips World' on Executions." http://news.bbc.co.uk/1/hi/world/asia-pacific/1425570.stm.
34. Ian Black, "Amnesty Demands Iran End 'Grotesque' Stoning Executions," *Guardian*, January 15, 2008. www.guardian.co.uk/world/2008/jan/15/iran.
35. *Daily Times* (Pakistan), editorial, January 30, 2007. www.dailytimes.com.pk/default.asp?page=2007%5C01%5C30%5Cstory_30-1-2007_pg3_1.
36. Amnesty International, *The State of the World's Human Rights*,

2008. www.amnesty.org/en/library/asset/MDE14/014/2007/ en/dom-MDE140142007en.html.

37. Quoted in *Washington Post*, "Capital Punishment Returns to Iraq: Public Welcomes Practice Suspended After U.S. Invasion," May 26, 2005, p. 16.

Chapter 1: The History of the Death Penalty

1. How did religious scriptures like the Bible and the Koran influence societies throughout history as they formulated policy on capital punishment?
2. Why did Cesare Beccaria oppose the death penalty?
3. What did execution victims Socrates, Joan of Arc, and Sacco and Vanzetti all have in common?

Chapter 2: Arguments for the Death Penalty

1. "If the majority of Americans support the death penalty, it should be the law of the land." Do you agree? Why or why not?
2. How do supporters of the death penalty counter the statistics that show execution costs the state more than life imprisonment?
3. Which of the eight arguments in favor of capital punishment (highlighted in a sidebar in the chapter) seem the strongest to you, and why?

Chapter 3: Objections to the Death Penalty

1. Explain the "brutalization" theory.
2. How do supporters of capital punishment justify the execution of innocent people?
3. How do we know that the death penalty is applied inconsistently?

Chapter 4: The Road to the Death Penalty in the United States

1. For the last forty years, what has been the trend of Supreme Court decisions about the death penalty?
2. How would you have decided the Supreme Court case of *McCleskey v. Kemp*?

3. How has the victims' rights movement affected opinions about capital punishment?

Chapter 5: The Death Penalty Around the Globe

1. How does the death penalty in the United States differ from the death penalty in the four countries that execute more people than the United States does (China, Iran, Saudi Arabia, and Pakistan)?
2. Why do the people and the government of Singapore support capital punishment?
3. Do you think that the death penalty will ever be abolished around the world? Why or why not?

ORGANIZATIONS TO CONTACT

Amnesty International USA
5 Penn Plaza, 16th Fl.
New York, NY 10001
phone: (212) 807-8400
Web site: www.amnestyusa.org

Amnesty International is a worldwide movement of 2.2 million people who campaign for internationally recognized human rights for all. It tracks human rights abuses worldwide and reports on them; its Web site publicizes thoroughly the use of the death penalty, which it opposes, country by country.

The Death Penalty Information Center
1101 Vermont Ave. NW, Ste. 701
Washington, DC 20005
phone: (202) 289-2275
Web site: www.deathpenaltyinfo.org

The Death Penalty Information Center is a nonprofit organization serving the media and the public with analysis and information on issues concerning capital punishment. The center was founded in 1990 and prepares in-depth reports, issues press releases, conducts briefings for journalists, and serves as a resource to those working on this issue. The center is widely quoted and consulted by all those concerned with the death penalty. The center offers information but not opinions.

Justice for All
PO Box 55159
Houston, TX 77255
phone: (713) 935-9300
Web sites: www.jfa.net • www.prodeathpenalty.com

Justice for All defines its mission as advocacy for change in a criminal justice system that is inadequate in protecting the lives and property of law-abiding citizens. It maintains the www.prodeathpenalty.com site that updates information on capital cases and sponsors local chapters that can be formed by calling the office in Texas.

National Center for Victims of Crime
200 M St. NW, Ste. 480
Washington, DC 20036
phone: (202) 467-8700
Web site: www.ncvc.org

The National Center for Victims of Crime is the nation's leading resource for crime victims, including the families of murder victims. Its Web site provides links to dozens of pro–death penalty articles and resources.

Students Against the Death Penalty
1600 Wickersham Ln., #3084
Austin, TX 78741
phone: (210) 601-7231
Web site: www.studentabolition.org

Students Against the Death Penalty (SADP) works to end the death penalty through campaigns of public education and the promotion of youth activism. SADP is an all-volunteer, grassroots organization formed in 2006 with the primary goal of mobilizing national support for a moratorium on executions and/or abolition of the death penalty

Books

Robert N. Baird and Stuart E. Rosenbaum, *Punishment and the Death Penalty: The Current Debate*. Amherst, NY: Prometheus, 1995. A collection of twenty short essays by leading theorists on both sides of the capital punishment issue.

Lauri S. Friedman, ed., *Opposing Viewpoints: The Death Penalty*. Detroit, MI: Greenhaven, 2007. Twenty brief essays by experts, grouped thematically: "Is the Death Penalty Just?" "Is the Death Penalty Effective?" and so forth.

Gary P. Gershman, *Death Penalty on Trial: A Handbook of Cases, Laws and Documents*. Santa Barbara, CA: ABC-CLIO, 2005. A comprehensive set of source materials, including short selections from Supreme Court justices' opinions.

Ted Gottfried, *The Death Penalty: Justice or Legalized Murder?* Brookfield, CT: Millbrook, 2002. Stories of death row inmates and victims, in an engrossing narrative style with commentaries on both sides of the issue.

Harry Henderson, *Capital Punishment*. New York: Facts On File, 2000. From the Library in a Book series, this book provides a comprehensive study of the death penalty, including a chronology of Supreme Court death penalty cases and chapters on the history of capital punishment and the death penalty abroad.

John W. Weier, *Capital Punishment: Cruel and Unusual?* Detroit: Gale/Cengage, 2006. A collection with helpful features, including Supreme Court cases grouped by death penalty subtopics, charts and graphs, and state-by-state updates.

Web Sites

American Civil Liberties Union (www.aclu.org/capital/general/10441pub19971231.html). A division of the left-wing, liberal ACLU Web site devoted to data and essays organized by abolition arguments ("Capital Punishment Is Barbarous," "Capital Punishment Is Unfair," and so forth).

Death Penalty Information Center (http://deathpenaltyinfo.org). The largest and most comprehensive death penalty site online (with international links), that includes pro–death penalty information but, despite a disclaimer on the home page, is abolitionist.

National Center for Policy Analysis (www.ncpa.org/pi/crime/ crime33b.html#E). The pro–death penalty section of a right-wing conservative site which posts essays supporting capital punishment.

Students Against the Death Penalty (www.studentabolition.org). An interactive, youth-oriented abolitionist site with YouTube videos, blogs, and photo montages.

U.S. Department of Justice, Bureau of Justice Statistics (www .ojp.usdoj.gov/bjs/cp.htm). Prints "Correction Statistics at a Glance" and other up-to-date information on executions and crime rates in the United States.

INDEX

PICTURE CREDITS

Cover image: Scott Olson/Getty Images
AP Images, 32, 35, 45, 55, 61, 62–63, 70, 73, 76–77, 80–81
© Bettmann/Corbis, 7, 25, 29
© The Bettmann Archive/Corbis, 10
© brt Photo/Alamy, 26
© Leonard de Selva/Corbis, 17
Getty Images, 47
© Mary Evans Picture Library/Alamy, 23
© Francis G. Mayer/Corbis, 15
© Bob Owen/San Antonio Express/ZUMA/Corbis, 50–51
© The Print Collector/Alamy, 12
© Thierry Roge/Reuters/Corbis, 79
Dibyangshu Sarkar/AFP/Getty Images, 87
© Christian Schmidt/zefa/Corbis, 37
© Shepard Sherbell/Corbis, 67
Roger Viollet/Getty Images, 20–21

ABOUT THE AUTHOR

Syd Golston is a school administrator, curriculum writer, and author. She has written materials for such programs and organizations as the PBS *Online NewsHour*, UNICEF, and the Commission on the Presidential Debates, and books about Apache women, Arizona history, and the Depression-era WPA guidebooks to the states. She is a social studies curriculum specialist for the Phoenix Union High School District and serves as president-elect of the National Council for the Social Studies. She lives in the desert foothills of Scottsdale, Arizona.